Baseball, Bobbleheads and Beyond

⊰⊱

By James L. Mullany

⊰⊱

BASEBALL, BOBBLEHEADS AND BEYOND

Copyright © 2018 by James L. Mullany

All rights reserved. Except as permitted under the U.S. Copyright Act of 1976, no part of this publication may be reproduced, distributed, or transmitted in any form or by any means, or stored in a database or retrieval system, without the prior written permission of the author.

ISBN:978-1798860663

TO MY DAUGHTERS ERIN AND ADRIENNE
AND
MY GRANDCHILDREN AVERY, CAMERON AND IAN

THESE STORIES ARE FOR YOU

*"Be true to the highest within your soul
and then always allow yourself to be governed
by no customs or conventions or arbitrary man-made rules
that are not founded upon principles."*
Ralph Waldo Emerson

Table of Contents

Introduction	1
Foreword – Illia Thompson	3
Baseball, Bobbleheads and beyond	5
Willie and Friends	7
A Ride Of A Lifetime	8
Kevin – Fifty Years Later	13
Childhood	17
Random Thoughts On My Youth	19
My Imperfection	23
A Defining Moment	26
Back To School Shopping – 1950's Style	28
A Modern Marvel	31
It's Howdy Doody Time	36
Coach Smith	39
Harrier 1962	43
Family	47
A Man I Once Knew	48
Dad, A Genuine Character	51
When Did You Last See Your Father?	60

Running In My Family	64
My Two Families	67
My Birth Family	67
My Married Family	80
I Left My Heart There	89
Where I Come From	91
19th Avenue, San Francisco	98
Kezar Stadium	102
Rincon Annex Post Office – San Francisco Of The 1960s	105
Passions	109
What Do I Need?	110
I Am Sorry But I Love Baseball	113
My Baseball Date	115
A Passion For Books	123
Bobbleheads	127
People	131
A Girl Named Erin	132
The Quiet Ones	137
Pinky, My Best Friend	145
The Mystery of Joe	148
Turning Points – Jacob Anderson	152
Uncle Gerald – A Family Eccentric	155
My Brother Mike	160

JOYS IN LIFE   171
    LADY – OUR PERFECT PET   172
    PEPPER   176
    THE GIFT – MY 18 SECONDS WITH JOE MONTANA   180
    THE ROLLING PIN   184
    COMFORT ZONES – MOVING TO PACIFIC GROVE   186

LIFE HAPPENS   191
    LEARNING TO SAY YES TO LIFE   192
    CHANGES IN MY LIFE   194
    THE MOMENT   198
    AN UNFINISHED LIFE CHANGES OVERNIGHT   202
    SOMETHING HAS HAPPENED   205
    TIS AN ILL WIND   208
    MY FRIEND DONALD; MAKING A DIFFERENCE   216
    LIFE AND DEATH – HOPE AND DESPAIR   220
    THE MYSTERY AND JOY OF LIFE   222

TRAVELS   239
    TRAVEL IS . . .   240
    TRAVELS WITH POP   242
    SPRING BREAK TRIP – FINDING MYSELF
        WITH MY DAUGHTERS   245
    IMMIGRANT – CALIFORNIA TO IRELAND   252
    THE GOOD SAMARITAN IN IRELAND   259

LETTERS TO MY GRANDCHILDREN   263
    BECOMING POPPA   264
    A LETTER TO AVERY   266
    A LETTER TO CAMERON   270
    A LETTER TO IAN JAMES   274

BEGINNINGS AND ENDINGS   279
    MY STORY – HITTING ROCK BOTTOM   260
    BEFORE I DIE I WANT TO (???)   286

ACKNOWLEDGMENTS   289

ABOUT THE AUTHOR   293

INTRODUCTION

I retired to Pacific Grove on the beautiful Monterey Peninsula in 2006 following my 38-year career with the State of California in San Francisco and Sacramento. I always loved the coast and it had been a dream of mine to retire there. One of my primary goals upon retirement was to write my family history or memoirs. My original idea was to do a genealogical family history tracing my ancestors back to Ireland.

With this in mind, I enrolled in Illia Thompson's Writing Class at the Sally Griffin Senior Center in Pacific Grove. I met others in the class who had similar goals and objectives; we wanted to pass on a part of ourselves and our life stories for our children and grandchildren. Many of us in the class regretted that our parents or grandparents had not left us some sort of documentation of their lives. I believe that as one nears the end of his or her life, we become more interested in those who came before us and who they were and the lives they lived. We want our children and grandchildren to know us and to leave a legacy for those who will follow.

I think of Illia Thompson more as a guide or facilitator than a teacher. She helped me find a way to mine my memories, to excavate and tell the stories that make up our lives. I even found my way to the Carmel Foundation in Carmel-By-The-Sea when Illia move her class to that location. I had started the class with the idea of writing a chronological history of my family ancestors and myself. But Illia's weekly prompts (or ideas for writing subjects) put me on a different course for telling my story. Our weekly essays about events in our lives, people we met along the way or memorable life experiences became the way I thought I could tell my story.

The essays in this collection are my stories. Some people in my life may remember details, dates or events differently, but these are the way I recall them and thus they are my stories. Hidden within these stories are the answers to some age-old questions: What was the purpose of my life? Was my life meaningful or special? Did I have an impact on others and what was the impact of others on me? While I did not discover a cure for cancer or solve the world's problems, like all of us, in a small way I think I may have had in impact on those around me that I may never have imagined. In those books of essays, I think that I have captured the essence of the events in my life that helped to make me the person I am.

    In class, Illia has told us that our classroom was a "safe place" to write and read our essays. At first I did not understand what she meant, but I learned that many in the classes wrote things about themselves that they had never revealed to others. In my case, writing and reading my essay about my depression was one of the hardest things I have ever done. I am so grateful for the support I received from others in the class, who told me that they had suffered from depression and understood how hard it was to write or read about it.

    I hope those who read these essays enjoy them as much as I enjoyed writing them. There are other essays I wrote that were not included in this book – so there just may be another book in the future!

Jim Mullany
February 2019

Foreword
By Illia Thompson, Writing Instructor,
Memoir Writing

For over twenty years, during weekly two-hour sessions we gather to read parts of our lives to each other. Following prompts such as poetry, essays, objects, news items, we find triggers to our own stories awaiting telling. Personal insights occur as we listen deeply as well share our words.

Through writing Memoirs, we become more visible to ourselves as well as offer others the opportunity to know us more fully. The gift of shared self arrives. Each session nourishes.

Jim/James, as appears on his name card, arrived in my Memoir class over a dozen years ago. He began as Jim, but he wanted to also be known James once his beloved grandson, Ian James Scarborough, entered the world. Tentatively he began to tell his life, beginning with memories from his San Francisco childhood, through school and work and marriage and parenthood, marital separation, and poignantly through the premature birth of a grandson, who now happily is well. Jim/James's travels to Ireland and personal encounters deftly describe his life for those fortunate enough to hear his words. Shamrocks as well as the San Francisco Giants hold his heart. Highlighted humor and pathos offer a well-rounded picture of his journey, a voyage deserving of illumination.

*Illia Thompson's Monday Writing Class
at the Carmel Foundation
"We are writers!"*

Baseball, Bobbleheads and Beyond

"I dislike modern memoirs. They are generally written by people who have either entirely lost their memories or have never done anything worth remembering."
Oscar Wilde

Willie Mays
"The Greatest Baseball Player of All Time"

WILLIE AND FRIENDS

This essay about my ride with Willie Mays appears first in this collection because it was the first essay of mine that was published. It appeared in the Neighbors section of the Sacramento Bee on July 15, 1993

"There have been two geniuses in the world.
Willie Mays and Willie Shakespeare."
Tallulah Bankhead

A Ride of a Lifetime

    The picture of Willie Mays waving to the 1993 opening day crowd at Candlestick Park from a convertible brought back poignant memories of a day thirty-five years ago. On that day, Willie and his pink Thunderbird made a dream come true for a thirteen-year-old boy – me.

    By the summer of 1958, like most boys my age in San Francisco I had become a devoted follower of the San Francisco Giants. The Giants had moved from New York earlier that spring, and "The City" was already in the grip of a love affair with its major league team.

    Throughout the city, fans of all ages were sporting new black baseball caps emblazoned with the orange "SF" logo. San Franciscans toted transistor radios on cable cars, to the opera and along Market Street to follow the progress of their team.

    The talk in our neighborhood centered around trips to Seals Stadium to view our heroes in person. In my circle of friends in the Parkside District, a friend named Kevin has captured our envy. Kevin's father had purchased two season tickets along the first-base side of the field. Kevin assured us that although his father believed that the tickets were for business clients, we would be able to use them as well during the summer. Kevin's reputation among his friends grew to almost mythic proportions when he casually mentioned to us that he regularly rode to and from the games with Willie Mays.

    The fact that a baseball superstar would routinely transport a kid to the ballpark strained our belief.

We sought to poke holes in Kevin's claim and challenged him to present us with evidence that he even knew the great Mays. Although we all secretly hoped that he was telling us the truth, our skepticism was strong.

Kevin told us that throughout the season he would take each one of us to a game and, if we were lucky, a ride with Willie might be arranged.

On that fateful day in July, a phone call from Kevin announced that it was my opportunity to accompany him to that afternoon's Giants-Phillies game.

My first question was, "What time is Willie going to pick us up?" Kevin advised me that we would be going to the game via the streetcar and the trolley. Before I could protest this arrangement, he assured me that a ride home from Willie was a possibility.

Our trip to Seals Stadium offered a brief reprieve from the fog that enshrouded our neighborhood, where sunshine was just a rumor during the summer months. Seals Stadium was the splendid predecessor of the infamous Candlestick Park. The stadium was an intimate ballpark bordered by a bakery, a brewery, and a small park. Fans were treated to the aroma of baking bread in a stadium that had a five-story neon beer glass looming over it from behind the home plate stands. The glass would fill up with sparkling neon beer constantly throughout the day and night.

Most of the game that day was a blur to me because all I could think of was the impending ride home. I focused my attention on Willie. He played the game with an exhilarating style that combined speed, power, and grace. He would run down fly balls in the outfield with his patented basket catch.

If there ever was a man who was born to play the game of baseball, this was the man. His name was one of the few that would be spoken with the reverence reserved for Ruth, Gehrig, DiMaggio, and Mantle.

When the game was over, we stationed ourselves in the players' parking lot behind the centerfield scoreboard. In those days, before million-dollar player contracts, players drove ordinary cars and they were not provided special security parking.

As we waited by Mays' pink Thunderbird (the first model with a back seat area), Kevin briefed me on the code of behavior that was expected in Mays' presence. Speak only when spoken to, don't ask for his autograph, and don't embarrass Mays with any childish behavior. In my mind, I feared that I was being set up for public humiliation by an elaborate practical joke, but in my heart, I prayed that I was wrong.

The moment quickly arrived when a swarm of kids came forward with Mays in their midst. His brow was furrowed, and the look of tension on his face told me that this man was not comfortable with his fame. In a quick motion, he dismissed the other kids and motioned Kevin to get into the front passenger seat. From the back seat, I looked out at the faces of the kids outside the car who stared at us with wonder and envy. I felt like a celebrity myself. I was riding in the car with the most famous ballplayer in America.

The 25-minute ride up 16th Street to Market Street and over the Twin Peaks hills passed in silence inside the car. However, outside the car there were horns honking in recognition. People would stop, smile and wave at the car. All I could do was sit in awe as I stared at the back of Willie's head.

Finally, I could no longer contain myself. I blurted out, "It was a tough day out there today, Willie." Willie glanced up at me in the rearview mirror and replied, "Son, the great thing about baseball is that there is always another game tomorrow."

We pulled into the garage of Mays' hillside home on Miraloma Drive, and it was all over. Before departing up the stairs, Willie told us to take an autographed picture from a box on the workbench and instructed us to close the garage door as we were leaving.

I walked the two miles back to our neighborhood with Kevin, but to this day I'm not certain if my feet actually touched the ground. One of the greatest baseball players of all time had given me the ride of a lifetime.

Willies Mays
"The Greatest Baseball Player of All Time"

"The Catch"

Willie Mays - The Greatest to Ever Play

Willie Mays at Seals Stadium in San Francisco – 1958

KEVIN – FIFTY YEARS LATER

April 30, 2018

    In the summer of 1993, I submitted an essay to the Sacramento Bee about my ride with the baseball legend Willie Mays when I was a kid. The Thursday supplement of the paper, called the Neighbors section, had a feature called "My Story", in which readers could submit a personal story for publication. I thought I had a good story about getting a ride with William Mays when I was a boy back in 1959 in San Francisco. The paper selected my story and I had my photo taken to accompany the story. I was given a $25.00 check, so I could say that was my first and only professional writing job. I had a very positive response from friends and family.

    The essay involved a friend of mine named Kevin who, as a ten-year-old boy, managed to strike up a friendship with Willie that included regular rides from Seals Stadium, the first home of the San Francisco Giants, for Kevin and whomever he took to the game with him. I was extremely fortunate to once receive a ride from the ballpark with Kevin and the legendary Mays. I called my essay "Say Hey, Willie, Thanks for the Ride of a Lifetime". I later sent the article to Willie and he signed it, along with sending me an autographed picture. Most of America knew what had happened to Willie – he set all-time baseball records, was elected to the Baseball Hall of Fame, and became generally recognized as the greatest baseball player of all time. But what about the co-star of that occasion – Kevin? What had become of him? Although Kevin had lived down the street from me on 19th Avenue in San Francisco and we attended the same high school, over time we lost track of each other.

    A few years after the publication of the article, I attended the funeral of the mother of a friend from San Francisco, where I encountered Kevin's mom who still lived in the old Parkside neighborhood. We caught up with old times, talking about neighborhood people. She told me that Kevin had achieved a bit a fame himself in high school and college playing basketball at Santa Clara University, where he had helped lead his team to be one of the top teams in the country. After college, he went on to a career as coach and teacher at the high school level in the Bay Area. I told her that I had written an article about us getting a ride with Willie Mays. She said Kevin would enjoy reading it and she would pass along a copy of the article to him.

So, the late 1990s was about the end of the contact I had with Kevin's family. Earlier this year (2018) I read an article in the San Francisco Herald that at my old high school in San Francisco, there had been a major renovation of the school gymnasium and basketball court. The article mentioned that the basketball arena was going to be named after another Kevin – Kevin Restani, who had gone on to play professional basketball and died suddenly in his early 50s while playing recreational basketball at the Olympic Club in San Francisco. A fundraising drive with a generous donation from the Olympic Club made the project possible. The article went on to describe some of the history of the school and the prominent basketball players and coaches who had played and coached in that gym. They mentioned my friend Kevin Eagleson as one who not only earned basketball honors there, but had coached the basketball team for seven years, achieving one of the greatest records in the school's history. In addition to getting a scholarship to Santa Clara University, he also was a member of the school's athletic Hall of Fame. I decided I would try to make contact with Kevin and maybe get together with him.

I Googled his name, and I was quite surprised to learn he was currently teaching and coaching at Palma School in Salinas, just a few miles away from my home in Pacific Grove. I e-mailed him via the school and received a response the very next day. Kevin wrote me that after many years of teaching, coaching, and being a principal of schools in San Jose, for the past three years he had been teaching in Salinas and now lived on the border of Monterey and Pacific Grove. He said that the prior evening he'd had dinner in Pacific Grove and probably had driven by my house on Lighthouse Avenue! It was amazing that we had lived a half a block away from each other in San Francisco about a half a century ago, and now we were living about two miles apart on the Monterey Peninsula. We made arrangements to meet for lunch.

I learned from the Internet that Kevin was an exceptional person, too. At the 125th anniversary of the Santa Clara Alumni Association, Kevin was recognized as the male Alumnus of the Year. The award recognized him for his outstanding service to humanity, and specifically recognized this alumnus who lived the ideals of competence, conscience and compassion. Besides his basketball playing and couching achievements, he gave up the big potential income of a college coach to devote himself to inner-city education as a teacher and a principal. One of his teachers said he significantly improved the academics in a school where the majority of the students fell below the poverty line, and he had opened his home to several students, welcoming them to stay with his own family for long periods of time. He and his wife Diane became surrogate parents for many of his students.

When I got together with Kevin for a three-hour lunch of pizza and a long walk down memory lane, we talked of friends, family, and our old neighborhood in San Francisco. We shared our viewpoint of our good fortune at being raised in the Parkside area of San Francisco in the good times, where all the families knew each other. We lived across the street from a park that had a playground, athletic fields, basketball and tennis courts, and later a swimming pool. Around the corner was our grammar school, which we both attended for eight years and spent many hours playing sports under the schoolyard lights. We shared stories about our neighborhood, where few people locked their doors and many families had no idea where the keys to their house were located. (I recall once my father was so occupied by reading the newspaper, he erroneously entered our neighbor's house, where he sat down in the living room and continued to read the newspaper.) Kevin said his mother used to leave the kids' lunches on the dining room table when she had to be out at lunch time. Kevin learned of a classmate of his who often preferred Kevin's mom's lunches to his own. So, the kid would race from school to Kevin's house and grab Kevin's lunch before Kevin got home. Kevin said for months he had blamed his brothers for stealing his lunch.

Kevin told a story that shows how baseball and writing can link people. He said he had once told some students that he had been friends with Willie Mays. Some of his students were skeptical and wanted Kevin to prove it, so Kevin said he brought a personalized Willie Mays bat that Willie had signed for him and a copy of the essay I had written. The students said the essay I had written convinced them that Kevin had indeed known the great Willie Mays.

I told Kevin that I had been attending a writing class in Pacific Grove and Carmel for years and that I was in the process of putting together a book of the essays I had written. I informed him that the very first essay in the book would be the Willie Mays story, and I thanked him for his role in my writing. I said that I had searched for an appropriate quote to introduce each essay; the one for the Willie Mays essay came from, of all people, Tallulah Bankhead:

*"There have been two geniuses in the world –
Willie Mays and Willie Shakespeare."*
ಸಿಂಚ

Kevin and Jim

CHILDHOOD

"You never forget the neighborhood kids you grow up with."
                                        Unknown

"Before I had children I had five theories of child rearing. Now I have five children, and no theories."
                                        Unknown

St. Cecelia's Kindergarten class
San Francisco, 1950

Jim

Random Thoughts On My Youth

It is said that youth is wasted on the young. I contemplate this and I wonder and I think of my youth.

The baby of the family – number five of five. James, Jimmy, and Jim, sharing those names with my father and grandfather, fortunately not a junior or not the third.

Born just at the end of WWII, too young to be one of the greatest generations, too old to be a baby boomer, just a kid of the 50s, not the 60s.

Encased in a cast from my chest to my toes for almost two years to straighten out my leg. Now this problem is corrected by special shoes or a brace.

For boys like me, it was plastic green army men, cowboys and Indians and flexi flyers.

Davy Crocket Coonskin Caps were a popular fad in the 1950s

Hand-me-down clothing and sports equipment from my older brother; playing first baseman on teams solely because I only had a first-baseman's glove.

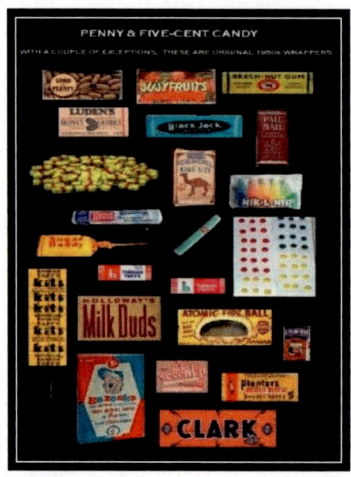

Penny Candy was a big favorite at Variety Store

My Favorite - Circus Peanuts

Sandlot baseball, penny candy, trips to the five-and-dime and soda fountains.

A TV with rabbit ears – It's Howdy Doody Time, Hi Ho Silver Away, a member of the peanut gallery, Roy and Dale, Hopalong Cassidy, and sidekicks named Gabby or Tonto.

*On Saturdays in San Francisco
the local TV channel
showed Westerns*

Changing the television channels before there were no remote controls; so, as the youngest in the family, I was a human remote control. "Jimmy, please turn the channel to Uncle Miltie or Ed Sullivan."

Saturday afternoons at the Parkside Theater in our neighborhood; it was Saturday for kiddy matinees with seventeen cartoons and comedies – Ma and Pa Kettle, Francis the Talking Mule, Martin and Lewis, Flash Gordon - for ten cents or five cereal box tops. And it was only kids – no adults.

Collecting baseball cards and actually liking the gum that came in the packets.

It was Elvis on the top forty radio channel – "Don't Be Cruel," "You Ain't Nothing But A Hound Dog," "Blue Suede Shoes" and "Jailhouse Rock".

It was a time for lining up for polio vaccine shots and being relieved when they switched to sugar cubes.

It was the cold war, bomb shelters and surviving a nuclear attack by getting under your desk.

It was movie theater experiences at The Fox, The Warfield, The Empire and The El Rey and other grand movie palaces.

A visit to "Painless Parker", the economy doctor on Sutter Street and learning first hand why he was an economy doctor.

It was St. Cecilia's school wearing a uniform, always addressing my teachers as **Sister!**

It was being an altar boy, learning Latin responses and the smell of incense at Mass.

It was Thursday dancing lesson at school with Mrs. Hunter, which I hated, and just being terrified of having to dance with girls.

It was your mother telling you to stay out of the house until dinner time, not being underfoot and just giving your parents some peace and quiet.

It was a time without children's car seats and seat belts, child-proof caps, a time of unsafe playground equipment and play structures, climbing trees without a net; it was a time to be a kid – and most of us not only survived but we actually thrived.

My Imperfection

I have heard and read that my particular imperfection might cause me to die early, to make it more likely that I will go insane, will make me more easily scared, and to more likely cause me to be physically and mentally confused at school. In addition, because of this imperfection, I am likely to be regarded as evil, different, odd and weird. In fact, the Latin derivation of the word to describe my imperfection is *sinistra* or sinister. Look up the definition for the term describing my imperfection in the Oxford English Dictionary and some of the definitions you will find are "crippled," "defective," "awkward," and "illegitimate." Better yet in the French language, the term used to describe my imperfection is defined as crooked and ugly, while the word in Italian is defined as disfigured or dishonest. It was my father who first informed me of my great misfortune of having this imperfection when he said to me, **"Jim, I hate to tell you this, but you are a left-handed person in a right-handed world."**

So, like hundreds of thousands of kids raised in the 1940s and 50s, my parents worked to correct my imperfection of being left-handed in a right-handed world by "converting" me from a left-hander to a righty. I think most parents of this era were well-meaning and thought they were doing us a favor by making this conversion. But for many of us, the result was just more confusion and awkwardness. Being forced to use a hand which was not natural in some ways suppressed what was natural and only resulted in more confusion. In my case, I believe that at birth or a young age I was totally and completely a left-hander, but by the age of eight or nine years old, I was a right-hander in all things except handwriting and brushing my teeth. I am not sure why I remained a left-hander in only those two activities, but my parents were quite pleased that in all sports activities I was a right-hander. Of course, when it came time for new activities involving tools or utensils or in some fine motor activities, I seemed to be neither right- nor left-handed, just confused and awkward. My brain oftentimes could not decide which hand was to be dominant in these new activities. Although my parents never resorted to referring to my being left-handed as "evil or strange", for many years I felt that I was odd or different because I was a lefty.

If I had any doubts that it was a right-handed world, those doubts were emphatically removed by my experiences at school. From school desks to notebooks to blackboards to scissors to pencil sharpeners, everything in the classroom and school was either right-handed or oriented towards a right-handed world. Even learning the basics skill of handwriting and cursive was oriented and taught as if every student was right-handed, and to the best of my recollection, I never received any specific instruction on how to write left-handed. As a result, learning to write was a somewhat troubling and frustrating experience of twisting one's arm and hand or moving around the paper to various angles in order to replicate a right-handed orientation. I recall that much of my lifetime, I smeared ink onto my fingers and hand as I tried to write. As a shy kid, one of the most frustrating and terrifying experiences was being called upon to write on a chalkboard in front of a class. I recall literally shaking and sweating as I tried to figure out how to write on the blackboard without smearing chalk all over myself, as the chalk was usually worn out at an angle that seemed to be right-handed. To replicate the writing style on a flat surface, I sometimes thought that I would either have to twist my arm and body into an unattainable position or maybe ask the teacher if a chalkboard could be turned upside down.

Although I did ultimately develop my own sort of back-handed writing style that avoided the wrap-around writing style that was favored or adopted by many left-handed writers, I found out the worst experience of left-handed writing in high school and college was with those "right-handed desks" that required a tall left-handed writer to be a contortionist and twist like a pretzel in order to write at one of these desks. I recall a few long essay exams in college where I literally developed a full body cramp while completing my blue book exam. And the real insult of the experience was when a professor would inform me that my two-hour contortion experience had resulted in an examination paper that was illegible.

It is commonly believed that approximately seven to ten percent of the population is left-handed, but even that number is a rough estimate due to the number of people who are not truly dominant with either hand. There are many theories about what causes a person to be left-handed, but generally, it is just not known. The most prevalent theory is there is a right-handed gene and left-handed people are missing that gene, or more likely there is a combination of factors involving genes, hormones, evolutionary and environmental factors. In my case, I happened to marry a left-handed woman. We did not believe in "mixed marriages," and we had one totally dominant left-handed daughter and one totally dominant right-handed daughter. And then the ultimate irony, my left-handed daughter has two children who are right-handed, and my right-handed daughter has one son and, of course, he is left-handed. But fortunately for them, they came into a world of greater tolerance and understanding, a sort of kinder, gentler world for left-handers. A wonderful world of left-handed scissors, left-handed knives, left-handed kitchen utensils, left-handed notebooks and even a "little lefties" school and utensils sets for the young ones. So, I am so pleased to say that finally "Life now can be good for left-handers."

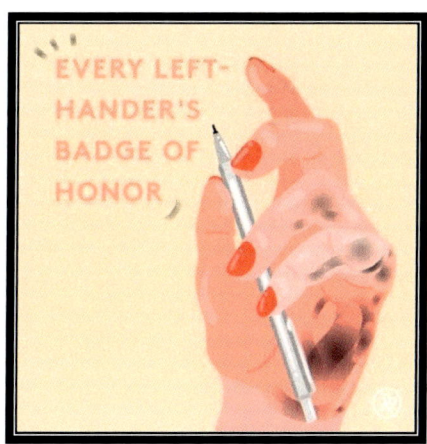

A Defining Moment

I was about eight or nine years old when it happened, and for a defining moment it is hazy and foggy in my mind to this day. In fact, I can only recall what came before it, and what came after it. But the actual moment is lost to me forever because it was not witnessed by others or me.

I was playing in the backyard of our house in San Francisco when I heard the call, the call of nature that is. Being that I was eight or nine, it made perfect sense to me to ignore the logical route of using the stairs to our family's one bathroom. No, for me it made perfect sense to climb the back porch's wooden supports to enter the home's second story like some kind of monkey cat burglar. I had used this route many times in the past. The last thing I remember is reaching far up to a lower railing to grasp in order to pull myself up to the deck of the porch.

The first thing I can recall after my ill-fated ascent is that I was in a very large strange bed, and I did not recognize anything about my surroundings. Where was I, and how had I gotten here? My head hurt a bit, but it really hurt when I tried to figure out where I was. Finally, a kind woman came to my bedside and explained to me that I was in a hospital and that I had fallen on my head. She told me there were two things I was forbidden from doing: the first was I was not to touch my head, and the second was that I was not to try to get out of bed without calling her for assistance. So, of course, the first thing I did was touch my head, to discover it felt like mush. After I had sufficiently explored in detail the condition of my head, I tried to get out of bed, and the last I can recall of that episode was the room spinning all around me.

When I next awoke I was back in bed, and the nurse and my parents were at my bedside, surrounding the bed and staring down at me. I figured I was in big trouble now, but then I suddenly realized that they were smiling at me, and just kept asking me over and over how I was feeling. In retrospect, as an adult and as a parent, I now fully understand how defining a moment that was, just from the looks on my parents' faces. Their looks were a combination of concern, worry, fear, and great relief, for I had come within inches of landing head first on some concrete steps that likely could have caused a significant brain injury or paralysis.

Although in the end, it did not turn out badly for me at all, because from that day forward, according to my older brothers and sisters, eating all our vegetables, keeping our rooms clean, and doing our chores were no longer as important to my parents as they had been in the past.

BACK TO SCHOOL SHOPPING – 1950S STYLE

"HE HAS NARROW FEET!" my mother would loudly announce to one and all as we entered the Sommer and Kauffman Shoe Store in Lakeside Village in San Francisco. It was the dreaded ritual of back-to-school shopping that my mother loudly proclaimed every August in the 1950s. Those words come back to me even today; whenever I pass by a shoe store, I expect a clerk to come running out and identify me as, "Hey, weren't you the kid with the narrow feet?"

All of these memories come flooding back to me simply by looking at a vintage photo of the young boy being measured for dress pants by a department store clerk as the boy's mother looks on seated nearby. The formal wear of the participants in this photo places the scene in the late 1940s or early 1950s. The assignment in our writing class was to pick a photo from the Reminisce Magazine and write about the memories the photo unleashed or triggered. The boy in the photo could have been me fifty years ago.

The clothes shopping segment of back-to-school shopping was relatively painless because I attended St. Cecilia's Parochial School and we had to wear school uniforms. That was just fine with me because the faster I could get out of the boys' clothing department of the Emporium store the better. I think I have always been a guy shopper at heart – get in, get what you need and get out. With the school uniforms, there was only minimal opportunity for my mother to embarrass me by having me model numerous styles of pants, sweaters or shirts. We had to wear forest green sweaters, charcoal colored corduroy pants and white shirts – although my mother did manage to cause a bit of embarrassment by calling the shirts blouses. Didn't she know, "Guys did not wear blouses, they wore shirts?"

But my mother surely made up for both the brevity of the shopping experience and the lack of my embarrassment when it came to the back-to-school shoe shopping experience. What should have been a relatively simple transaction of black or brown shoes for a ten-year-old boy became a long and excruciating shoe shopping marathon. It always started with her general pronouncement, **"He has narrow feet"** to any and all she encountered in the shoe store.

You first have to understand although my mother was a small woman, she had a very loud voice. In fact, both my parents and all my siblings were loud. I'm not sure if that was just the norm for large Irish families or if it was a survival technique in our family; to be heard you had to speak loudly. Being referred to as the quiet one in our family, as I often was, was definitely not a compliment, and was even looked upon by some of my older siblings as almost a genetic defect. All I know is my mother would garner the attention of sales clerks, customers, and especially other kids whenever she made her announcement in a shoe store.

Shoe stores back in those days seemed to employ a legion of managers, sales clerks, stock boys and others, each with an assigned specialty from measuring, evaluating, selling, retrieving and boxing shoes in a veritable assembly line process. So of course, my mother had to be sure that each and everyone knew that – **"he has narrow feet."** I am sure my mother did not intend to embarrass me, although she did seem to turn a deaf ear to my requests to not announce something I considered a personal embarrassment or a revelation of physical deformity, almost as if she would announce to my baseball buddies that I "threw like my sisters." I can still hear in my mind the endless echo of exchanges from sales person to stock clerk to boxers – **"He has narrow feet, he has narrow feet, he has narrow feet."**

I wonder why certain childhood memories of our parents persist while others just drift away. Is part of it the perceived embarrassments that all children seem to have inflicted upon them by parents? Or is it a psychological perception we have of long-lasting characteristics of our parents? I had once heard memory described as an analogy of chicken wire upon which mud is thrown, and most of the mud passes through while a small portion of the mud sticks. Just like with our memories, it is a mystery what sticks and what passes through. But life does seem to come full circle. I once overheard my two adult daughters talking about the times when I taught them to drive and I heard one of them mimicking a caution I gave them while they drove: **"You're drifting, you're drifting."** And it caused me to reflect – I wonder if they knew their father had narrow feet?

A Modern Marvel

Back in the early 1950s when I was growing up in San Francisco, the marvel of the ages was the development of television. I was convinced that our family of five kids was not only the last family on 19th Avenue to have a TV, we were quite possibly the last people in San Francisco to have one. I recall that our next-door neighbors, the Harrington's, became the most popular family in our neighborhood when they purchased the first television set I ever saw. All the kids in the neighborhood became "television friends" with the Harrington's. I am not sure how obvious it was to them, but our friendship with this family was solely for the purpose of getting an opportunity to watch the modern electronic marvel. It required us to swallow our pride, dignity and all principles in order to pretend that the only kid in the family, Lee, was actually a kid worth playing with.

All of our schemes and strategies had the objective of being able to watch our new-found friends in TV land with names like Howdy Doody, Beanie and Cecil, Kukla, Fran and Ollie, Fireman Frank, Dynamo Dudley, Captain Fortune, the Lone Ranger, and numerous shows.

The Lone Ranger Rides Again

    I think back in those days kids were more innocent and naive than the kids of today. We totally believed in the magic we saw on the screen. Simple puppets and marionettes were virtually indistinguishable from the real people who glowed from those large consoles with the tiny screens. We were mesmerized and transfixed by the fuzzy black and white images that were mysteriously transmitted to us. We would sometimes stare in a hypnotic-like trance at a test pattern for minutes on end just waiting for our shows to begin, never knowing how exact the scheduled starting time of a program would be adhered to on a particular day. I recall that television took over our lives in numerous ways; our games and activities came to a halt or our schedules were dictated by the schedule of our favorite programs. Games of sandlot baseball in the park ended abruptly whenever Howdy Doody was scheduled to commence. The world of kids was never the same once television entered our lives.

I believe there were times when my father struggled to support our family of five children on his postal clerk's salary, although I don't think we ever felt deprived. In retrospect, I now realize that many of the furnishings and appliances in our home were second hand or ones passed on from relatives or purchased at second-hand thrift shops. Our televisions were no different. Rather than fancy, large furniture consoles purchased from the large department stores like Sears, Penny's and Wards, our sets seemed to always be off-brand table models with undersized screens.

Ours carried names like Muntz, Philco, and Bendix. While the television sets of my friends and neighbors operated on the simple procedure of just turning a knob or pushing a button to operate the set, the operation of our set usually involved elaborate rituals. They might have included my father having to climb up to the roof in order to make intricate adjustments to our rooftop antenna while we screamed instructions up to him about the quality of the picture. Once the rooftop antenna had produced a reasonably clear picture, then there was the fine-tuning that involved the indoor rabbit ears antenna. This involved my father or one of the kids moving or rotating the antenna to find that perfect setting that would allow the clearest reception of a particular channel. Because of the hills, valleys, and winds in San Francisco, methods of achieving acceptable television reception became a virtual art form. As the youngest child in the family, I was sometimes assigned to be the "human antenna," where I had to position myself in a certain spot in order to either hold the rabbit ears in position or assume a pose that somehow made the picture on the TV much clearer.

My father loved to tinker and experiment with our television sets, and he had a great fascination with gadgets and gizmos that might enhance our viewing pleasure. I recall him bringing home a large, heavy sheet of thick magnifying glass with metal hooks to hook over our television screen to enlarge the picture. The glass was rounded in such a way that watching the screen produce large distorted images was like watching a television through a fishbowl. Later, when color television was developed, my father brought home what was our substitute for a genuine color TV. It was a sheet of clear plastic with some shades of color running through it that could be stuck onto the front of the screen like plastic wrap. The shades of color on the plastic, of course, never matched the actual color of the activity or characters on the screen, so we had to be the only family in America watching blue-faced cowboys riding red horses.

The ultimate television experience for our family was when my father actually made an appearance on television. One day while on his way to delivering the postal money order receipts to a downtown bank in San Francisco, my father was robbed in broad daylight. Apparently, the robber had mistaken my father's courier bag for a bank bag that contained cash, when all he was carrying was accounting paperwork. Back in those days, in San Francisco this "robbery" was noteworthy enough to make the local evening news. My father was interviewed by local newsman Fort Pearson, who asked my father to recount this ordeal. My father seized his opportunity to make the best of his few minutes of fame by grabbing the microphone from the startled reporter and doing a comedic monologue describing not only the robbery but also the ineptitude of the thief for picking a man who had only a scant fifty cents in his pocket (enough for carfare and soup for lunch), and the fact that was all the money his wife allowed him to carry to work in order to ensure enough money for food and clothing for his family of five children. Of course, my mother was mortified when his interview was broadcast that evening on the local news, while I think my father was always mystified that his performance did not lead to more television appearances for him.

It's Howdy Doody Time!

"Say, Kids, What Time is it?" "It's Howdy Doody Time!" Just seeing the words Howdy Doody written on the page and all these memories come flowing back to me like waters rushing unbridled over the falls. I am transported back to the early 1950s, about 4:00 pm every day and it was "It's Howdy Doody Time, Its Howdy Doody Time" sung along with the members of the peanut gallery on the small black and white television screen in our living room in our house on 19th Avenue in San Francisco. In our household, it was more than likely a second-hand, off-brand TV set like a Muntz or Philco. If my childhood can be defined by one show or one experience, it was this show. Every afternoon, I came in from playing outside – yes, <u>playing outside</u> as ordered by our parents is what we did in those days. Mothers all over our neighborhood ordered us outside, as in "go out and play and don't hang around this house." Our reprieve to come back into the house before dinner time was to view the Howdy Doody Show.

Back in those days, the kids' shows came on beginning around 4:00 pm and running until about 6:00 pm, during a time that was designated as children's hours. Broadcasts actually never seemed to be in sync back then as to when the proper viewing times would be and for what duration. Of course, that would not account for the time we stared at "test patterns," a screen device or picture that would be shown on the screen between programs. We would stare at this test pattern until our program came on the screen, which was very imprecise. A 4:00 pm show might start at any time from about 4:00 pm right on the dot to about 4:15 pm. In order to ensure we did not miss the beginning of the show, we just sat there staring at the screen until the show commenced. And back then, as far as I can recall, all the shows were in black and white, for it was only the rich people who had color televisions, and very few shows were broadcast in color.

Although these days I have trouble remembering what I had for breakfast or recalling that elusive password for my computer or ATM card, I recall the names of Buffalo Bob, Clarabelle the Clown, Indian Princess Summerfall Winterspring, the Indian Chief Thundercloud, who were real actors, and then the puppet or marionette characters who to me seemed just as real and genuine as the actors. There was Howdy Doody, the puppet boy dressed in western gear; Heidi Doody, Howdy's little sister; Mayor Phineas T. Bluster, which I always thought was the perfect name for a bag of hot air politician; the little pal named Dilly-Dally; and the very odd animal character who I could never quite figure out named Flub-a-Dub.

The half-hour shows never ceased to capture my attention and the attention of kids throughout the country. The genial, friendly Howdy and his pal Buffalo Bob were the hosts of the show. There was Clarabelle the Clown who communicated by honking a horn attached to his waist or by squirting other characters with water from his seltzer bottle. By today's standard, this show was primitive, simple and innocent. But I loved it. There was the bad guy or evil character Phineas T. Bluster, who was always concocting some evil scheme against one of the other characters; there was Flub-a-Dub, a pet that I later learned consisted of a combination of eight animals, such as a duck's bill, a cat's whiskers, a spaniel's ears, a giraffe's neck, a seal's flippers, etc.)

Although I did not realize it at the time, I think the show's names and use of language helped to lay the foundation for my love of words and reading. Howdy's name derived from the Western greeting of "How do you do." Bluster was a perfect name for a full-of-hot-air character; peanut gallery became part of the vernacular to mean a gathering of lesser characters or an audience. Flub-a-Dub was surely a mistaken creature of nature or a flub. I loved it all. It triggers my memory to recall all those entertaining shows of my childhood, from Crusader Rabbit, Hopalong Cassidy, the Cisco Kid, the Lone Ranger and Flash Gordon, Kukla, Fran and Ollie, and Fireman Frank. All shows that I fondly recall.

Coach Smith

It was the mid-1980s and I had stopped for gas at the service station in Sacramento, California when I first saw the man. I was in my early forties, and I was working as a Special Investigator for the Department of Employment. I observed a man talking with the attendant and there was something vaguely familiar about him. It was not his physical appearance that I recognized but more his essence, aura or spirit that I connected with. It was his gestures, the way he cocked his head to one side as he spoke and smiled at the attendant that registered with me. I moved closer and overheard the attendant inquiring about the man's license plate and the special "DP" designation on the plate. As the man explained, the "DP" on his license plate was a new designation on California license plates that identified the vehicle's owner as a "disabled person." I then knew who the man was, and I was astounded that I had recognized him some thirty years after I had last seen him. It was Coach Smith, my elementary school baseball and basketball coach at St. Cecilia's Grammar School in San Francisco.

"Are you Coach Darol Smith?" I asked. With a wide smile, he turned to me and replied, "Yes, I am Darol Smith, but I have not been called Coach Smith for many years." Before I was able to identify myself, Coach Smith pointed at me and gestured as if catching a baseball. "Jimmy Mullany, first baseman, St. Cecilia's, San Francisco CYO Champions from the fifties, the finest, the greatest and the best baseball team in Northern California." I was astounded that Coach Smith was able to recognize me from back then when I was an adolescent boy, and he even placed me back at my old position on the St. Cecilia's baseball team.

My memories quickly rewound and I was all the way back to San Francisco in 1955 when I was first tried out for the St. Cecilia's baseball team as a first baseman. It was my first attempt to play competitive sports. I tried out for the baseball team and first base was going to be my position solely because I had inherited my older brother's first baseman's baseball glove as a hand-me-down. I took the fact that I had a first baseman's mitt as a sign that I was destined to play the first baseman's position. Knowing that I would be playing first base, I actually recalled sleeping with that glove some nights because I read that was what some major-league players had done with their first gloves.

But it was Coach Darol Smith who made it all happen. I thought back to the day when the final roster for the team had been posted on the wall next to the entrance to the boys' bathroom at school. There had been about thirty or forty boys who had tried out for the team but only fifteen boys would be selected to be on the team because there were only fifteen uniforms available. I gathered with other boys to scan the list, and I was elated to see my name listed. The list was simple and did not expound beyond "the following boys have been selected for the St. Cecilia's baseball team." I quickly scanned the list. Among the names of the primarily Irish-Americans kids listed of Kennedy, Collins, McCoy, O'Boyle and Keating, there was my name – Jim Mullany, first baseman. There was disappointment for the boys who did not make the team; some resolved to work harder or to do better next time. But in the world of boys' sports back then, we trusted in the fairness of Coach Smith. We all knew that the fifteen boys listed had earned the honor of being on the team.

For each one of us had already served our apprenticeship of having competed and earned the respect of our peers on the playgrounds and local schoolyards in the cutthroat world of sandlot or baseball games. In the modern world of organized sports and Little League baseball, all was seemingly controlled by and set up for adults. The idea of games organized solely by kids, ruled totally by kids, and strictly for kids, is a dying or dead concept that thrived during the 1950s. In this world, as a young boy or the new kid to the game, you would be selected by and evaluated by "the big kids" or by your peers when teams were chosen. There was little sentiment, favoritism, politics or adult influence in this world of self-selection. Could you play or not play the game was the bottom line. Oh, there would be the occasional exception for the kid who might bring an essential piece of equipment like a ball, bat or glove into the mix, but even then, the kid would be aware that it was the piece of equipment that established his value or worth to the group. As one of the appointed captains might say with less than enthusiasm, "Okay, I'll take Tommy, but only because I like his Mickey Mantle bat."

In the world of boy's sandlot baseball, every aspect of the game was under the control of the kids, from the rules to the boundaries to the mediation of all disputes. There was the unspoken understanding of one rule above all others: It was absolutely forbidden to consult or request the involvement of any adult or parent to resolve any problem or dispute. A heated dispute or argument was resolved as simply as flipping a coin or a bat, or as extreme as threatening to quit and go home with the ball or the bat. It was understood that making a threat like "I'll tell my mother" might result in a boy being threatened with ejection from a game or from future games. We all agreed that the fun, beauty, and fairness of our game would be compromised or ruined if any adult or parent became involved.

We knew that once we had been elevated to a real team like the St. Cecilia's school teams, we could trust that Coach Smith would be fair and only select those boys who had earned their starting position on the team. Back in those days, the lives of kids were compartmentalized and separate from the adults. We had no idea how old Coach Smith was, what he did for a living or where he lived. He was just Coach Smith to us. I believe that he was the first adult I had encountered in my life who treated me as a person and not just as a kid. He taught us the fundamentals of the game, batting, catching and throwing, along with the nuances of anticipating where the ball would be going with the crack of the bat and the differences of positioning for a left-handed or a right-handed hitter. Although he taught us about the game of baseball, he also taught us many life lessons, such as the importance of practice and preparation, the respect one should have for an opponent, the importance of being focused in the moment and being both a good winner and a good loser. It was Coach Smith who planted in me the seeds of the passion for the game of baseball that grew to be my lifelong love. I guess you could say that everything that I needed to know and love about baseball I had learned from Coach Smith.

Epilogue:

Coach Smith later became a San Francisco police officer, and while assisting a stranded motorist, he was plowed into by a drunk driver, resulting in him losing a leg and receiving a disability retirement from the police department

HARRIER - 1962

In 1962, the fall of my senior year at Riordan High School in San Francisco, I was the number one harrier, or thin-clad, on the varsity. Part of my emergence to this esteemed position I attributed to the fartlek that I had done during the summer. Riordan High was an all-boys parochial school with an enrollment of about eight hundred students, and our team consisted of about twenty boys. I think if the term geek or nerd had been in use back then, we may have been identified as such; but in 1962 we were just considered different, or boys that marched to our own drumbeats. It turned out that we were actually pioneers in an activity that would later become a worldwide phenomenon. Our team was comprised of adolescent boys who were for the most part typical of the times, boys who would become government workers, teachers, businessmen, an alcoholic or two, but at the extremes there was one member of the team who would become a Congressman, while another would become one of the most notorious murderers in California history.

We were the Riordan High School Cross-Country running team. At the time, running was at best a fringe sport that in high school was considered an oddity and was in some instances used as a form of punishment in other sports. The reasons we were running on the cross-country team varied, from the one I used – I was getting in shape for another sport – while others just wanted to participate on a team. But the reality for most of us was that we knew everyone who just showed up for practice was on the team. There were no cuts or competition for places on the team, and each of us simply loved to run, which was not considered to be socially acceptable or cool back then.

The sport, its equipment, and the appearance of its participants contributed to the image of the oddness of cross-country running. First, we were a team in name only, as for the most part we trained as individuals and came together at competitive meets, where the highest placing of the first four or five runners on the team would have our placing added up to determine the team's score, with the lowest team score winning. Most of us were skinny, ectomorphic body types, and our "uniform" consisted of a white cotton t-shirt and shorts. We were often reminded that our team was a bunch of unathletic looking teenage boys running around in our underwear. Back in those days, there were only two running shoe brands and they were virtually impossible to find in American stores – Adidas and Puma. To find these shoes, you had to either do a mail order purchase from Germany or find a mysterious independent contractor selling the shoes from the trunk of a car.

Running cross-country in San Francisco was almost like an oxymoron, as cross-country courses are generally laid out in open woodland areas, run over rolling terrains with frequent sharp turns and variations in landscape laid out to be a severe test for runners. Courses also often included natural and artificial obstacles with markings that included tape, ribbons, chalk or paint markings to indicate the direction for runners. In high school in the early 1960s, it was believed that high school boys should never run more than two and a half miles. Those of us high school cross-country runners in San Francisco in the 1960s were blessed with a challenging course in one of the most beautiful urban parks in America – the legendary Golden Gate Park course. In two miles, the course challenged runners with every type of terrain and condition from calf-torturing sand pits, to equestrian trails with horse droppings to be maneuvered around, to blind curves through the heavy brush, to the wide-open 1,000-yard open meadow that finished with a 1,000-yard dash to the large oak tree in the center of Speedway Meadow.

Along the way, runners would encounter the SF Police Department horse stables, the paddock enclosure of the astounding bison herd that had been established in the park in the 1890s, pass the fly-fishing pond where anglers could practice their fly-fishing technique, on through the huge polo field where the wealthy socialites of San Francisco could park their luxury cars along the track to watch their friends in polo matches from the comfort of their automobiles. Some races might even encounter film stars Karl Malden and Michael Douglas filming the network television series "The Streets of San Francisco." Or in that final straightaway of the meadow, a runner might have to hurdle a human obstacle of a lounging/or napping beatnik from nearby Haight Ashbury "on the grass."

For me, the great thrill of cross-country running was leading a pack of runners to that meadow and wondering if my legs were strong enough to hold off the challengers that I could hear breathing heavily behind me. It was a thrill to finish in first place and to be handed the coveted Popsicle stick with the bold numeral "1" on it. The Popsicle sticks were later collected and the numbers added up to determine our team's placement. Yes, it was truly an "individual team sport."

The landscape of the world of running dramatically changed in the next ten years. First, there was the landmark research conducted by Dr. Kenneth Cooper, who observed the value of aerobic exercise for physical fitness, the recognition of Marathoner Frank Shorter of the United States who won the Olympic marathon in 1968, and finally, the founding of a new company by an Oregon cross-country runner and his coach, Nike, whose first shoe design happened because the coach had trouble finding the correct well-made shoes for his athletes so he began designing shoes for them himself. Running was no longer in the shadows; athletes all over the world were running in their underwear. It became an acceptable form of exercise by the late 1960s.

My infamous teammate? He was Dan White, two years behind me at Riordan High School and always behind me in cross-country races. He was expelled from Riordan High School one year after I had graduated. In 1978, Dan White assassinated the Mayor of San Francisco, George Moscone, and Supervisor Harvey Milk. White turned himself in to the San Francisco Police Department the same day, and he was later convicted of manslaughter when his defense team claimed his ingestion of fast foods and sugary snacks had diminished his capacity to form criminal intent to murder. White's defense became known as the "Twinkie defense." He was found guilty of manslaughter and served five years of his seven-year sentence in Soledad prison. About two years after his release from prison, he committed suicide.

Harriers starting a Cross Country Race in Golden Gate Park in San Francisco

FAMILY

*"You can't choose your family.
But you can choose to ignore their phone calls."*
From a greeting card

A Man I Once Knew

Andre Dubus III, the author of *The House of Sand and Fog*, was interviewed about his writing and his life and was asked to provide his favorite quotes about writing. Dubus said he had three separate quotes that had to go together:

Sarah Jewett: *"Write what you know."*
E.L. Doctorow: *"How do you know what you know?"*
Grace Paley: *"We write what we don't know that we know."*

Think about that. How profound and true those words are. And he adds another quote from Janet Burroway: "Writing isn't hard, not writing is hard," which Dubus says is a true test of knowing you are a writer.

Dubos's book *The House of Sand and Fog* is one of my favorite novels Its plot centers on a dispute over the ownership of a house between an Iranian immigrant family and a single woman who is a recovering drug addict. The story is profound, powerful, disturbing and dark. I think I was originally attracted to this novel by its title and its setting in Pacifica, California, where I had often visited as a child and where I had lived for three years as an adult. The title was a perfect description of the Pacifica I knew – a place of Sand and Fog. I was just amazed that Dubus, an easterner from Boston, was so able to capture the essence of Pacifica in his novel.

What fascinated me most about Dubus III was that he grew up in the shadow of his father, Andre Dubus, a critically acclaimed and adored short story writer. Young Andre said he did not know his father well growing up as his parents were divorced when he was young and added that he had not set out to be a writer. But having the name of a somewhat famous father was very difficult for him because he felt he had to work harder to establish his own identity apart from the father and find his own his own path to emerge from his father's shadow. He said he dealt with years of having his writings rejected and constantly being asked not about his own writings, but about his father's.

Being in the shadow of one's father (and a brother) was a subject that I was very familiar with. I was the youngest of five children, and the great age span between my older siblings and myself has always made me wonder if I was "an accident." My oldest sister is fourteen years older than me, and my brother, who is the fourth child in the family, is more than four years older than me. When it came to naming me, my parents took the easy way out, they named me James Leo Mullany, and I was about the fifth or sixth James in the immediate family; my maternal grandfather was James, my first cousin was James, and oh yes, my father was James Mullany. But in order to provide me with some distinction and individuality, I was James LEO Mullany while my father was James JOSEPH Mullany. This spared me from being a Junior, but I was to find out most people do not pay attention to middle names when two people's first and last names are the same.

Although my father was not famous or a celebrity, he was known within our local circle of friends, neighbors, merchants, and relatives in San Francisco and by his co-workers and acquaintances at and through his job with the Postal Service.

James JOSEPH Mullany was the person who came to mind when I read a quote from the 1890s when a street character addressed the San Francisco Board of Supervisors:

"Gentleman, as I look all of you over, I see that anyone can become a millionaire, but how many of you have the talent to become a character such as myself?"

I think my father could have comfortably addressed the Board of Supervisors or the US Congress in such a way had he been given the opportunity.

Dad was a one of a kind, throw away the mold, you don't see one like him everyday sort of man. He was an original, a piece of work, a true San Francisco character from the early 1900s where it was something of a distinction to be a character. He was a complex man in a rather simple package. He defied categorization or labels because he was so full of contradictions. And I believe he worked hard to fully develop those contradictions. He was an enigma, a mystery, a riddle and an eccentric character in an era when eccentric characters were admired. He could be a witty storytelling entertainer; a belligerent instigator of family disputes; a sentimental romantic giving his daughters candy on Valentine's Day; or a stubborn non-conformist who refused to open his Christmas presents on Christmas morning; an abrasive, opinionated man who could express bigoted words, yet would help persons of any race who were stranded on the road or needed help; a charming, lovable companion who would loan you his last dollar and come to your aid in the middle of the night; or a blissfully contented loner who napped on a deserted beach; or a mean-spirited drunk who wasn't happy until he had everyone at a party upset or in tears; a loving grandfather unselfishly caring for his grandchildren for hours and hours; or the man who took perverse delight in hearing about the first reported domestic dispute on Christmas morning on his police scanner. He was a man you could love or you could despise, sometimes even at the same time.

And I shared the name James Mullany with this man. And did it make my life interesting!

DAD – A GENUINE CHARACTER

My dad, James Mullany, a novice deckhand aboard a freighter at age 21 in 1926.

*Our job in this lifetime is not to shape ourselves into some ideal
we imagine we ought to be, but to find out
who we really are and become it.*
                                            Steven Pressfield

    I always thought of my father as a genuine character, partly because so many people I encountered called him that, as in "you know, your father is quite a character." In my early life, I was not really sure if that was a good or a bad thing. As I got older, I too came to think of him as a character. A character is one of those things in life that it is hard to define, but you know it when you see it.

    A bit about my father: He was an identical twin born in San Francisco in 1905 to Irish immigrant parents. He was one of eight boys and he had a sister who died as an infant before he was born. His father, Michael, had a coal and wood delivery business that, when my father was a small boy, was a horse-drawn wagon operation that in the early 1900s was converted over to a truck and wagon service. My father joked that his parents had eight boys primarily as a cheap source of labor for his father's business, as all the boys were expected to work in the family business. He always talked about how easy his kids had it, not having to clean out horse stalls and load wood and coal onto a wagon as he and his brothers had to do.

    I think my dad was somewhat shaped by his family environment, but also by the events he lived through in his lifetime. First, there was the 1906 Earthquake and Fire that caused significant damage to the Mullany family home and business; he lived through World War I, Prohibition, the Great Depression, World War II. He was very proud of the fact it was his generation that built the Golden Gate and Bay Bridges in San Francisco and rebuilt San Francisco after the earthquake, and he proudly pointed out that the Golden Gate Bridge, one of the world's great engineering achievements, was built to last forever.

Although he had been too young to serve in World War I and as he said, "was too old and had too many kids" to serve in World War II, he took great pride in being a member of what has been referred to as the Greatest Generation. He worked for about fifty years for the US Postal Service. He was an Irish-Catholic who claimed to have married the most beautiful girl in St. John's Parish. They had five kids over the span of eleven years from the mid-1930's to the mid-1940s.

As the youngest child in the family, my first memory of my father was when he was in his mid-forties. He was a hands-on parent with his kids, as he frequently would take us on outings to get us out of the house and give my mother time to not have kids underfoot and give her some of her own space. I have always wondered whether my dad worked at being a character or if he just evolved into one from his life experiences. He had a couple of eccentric brothers, so I am pretty sure some of his being a character was genetic.

A few examples: my dad was an opinionated close talker. By that I mean he loved to express his opinions to service station attendants, store clerks, and complete strangers. He seldom followed the general norms of society in terms of the space he left between himself and the people he encountered or accosted. First was the fact everyone was a kid to him. Whether a person was six or ninety, his usual greeting was, "Hiya kid," and as he moved in closer to his subject, the subject would back away from him. A frequent topic was lecturing about how everything a person could want or need was in San Francisco – my dad was a lifelong resident of San Francisco and he expected everyone to love it as much as he did. He loved to debate the attributes of The City against every other place; he loved to do this routine with immigrants who might have fond memories of their old country. Of course, except for a short stint as a merchant seaman, he seldom had traveled farther than the San Francisco Bay Area.

My dad had great respect for the workplace; having lived through the depression he valued his job and the fact it enabled him to support his family, which was expected of men of his era. Every day of his working life, he wore a gray suit, pressed white shirt, subdued colored tie, and polished dress shoes. I remember in my young life, he always wore a fedora as that was the expected "uniform" of the business community in The City. But at home, it was a different uniform he donned. He always wore a long-sleeved plaid shirt, gray work pants and a variety of work shoes or boots. Some of the plaid shirts looked like the wool Pendleton variety, but his were always a more inexpensive Montgomery Ward imitation version that he received every Christmas. He would never open these packages on Christmas morning but would leave them wrapped until weeks or months later and then opened them whenever he felt he needed a new one. The newer shirts would first become his dress shirt for social occasions, and the older ones would be relegated as work shirts as they aged. When the practice of wearing fedoras for work faded, the old hats became part of his casual outfit. He combed his full head of hair straight back exactly as he had worn it in his high school graduation photo. It was a style popular in the 1920s, so my dad often looked like a modern version of Jimmy Cagney or Leo Gorcey of the Dead-End Kids movies. I think the fact his wardrobe was always twenty to thirty years out of style was a source of pride and a mark of distinction to him.

You combine this look with the fact that he drove barely road-worthy Dodge, Buick and DeSoto cars that were also twenty to thirty years old, and you have something of the image he created. He never could afford to take his cars to a mechanic, so he usually repaired them himself, even though each repair job seemed to be a new one on him. For example, once when he could not find one of the cotter pins to remount a wheel, he ad-libbed the job with one of my sister's bobby pins. When the wheel later flew off when my brother had borrowed the car to drive a date to movies, he just chuckled and said that he guessed bobby pins were not as strong as he thought they were.

One of my father's hobbies was fishing, and for a week every year, he and his cronies – his old friends and his twin brother – would take a fishing trip up to the Mendocino Coast to Fort Bragg and vicinity. Oh, by way, we learned late in his life that my father had failed to renew his driver's license and drove without one for about thirty years. He somehow managed to share his twin brother's license whenever one was called for. That all ended in the sixties when he was stopped by the police for a moving violation, and he had my son-in-law, who was a police officer, get the ticket dismissed. But one day when his old Dodge was totally plastered with tickets from Officer Devine, he got the point and finally renewed his license at DMV, commenting the test had not changed much since the 1940s.

My father was a devoted letter and card writer – he even had a pen name, Gilbert Sullivan – as he was a devoted fan of the light operas of Gilbert and Sullivan. He loved to send and receive postcards, which I always thought was fitting for a man who worked his entire life for the postal service. But his technique was to write his postcards before he left for the trip, as we would see him making out the cards the evening before the trip. He said that he was usually "too busy" on his trips to spend time writing cards. My mother claimed much of these trips were spent drinking with his pals and that was why he was busy. A clue to this was the gallon jugs of "Dago Red" he loaded in the car with his fishing gear.

Having accompanied my dad on some fishing trips, I knew that he was an accomplished fisherman; he preferred to fish from the coastal shore or from piers, although on his annual trips he went out on rivers and the ocean on fishing boats. But he always wanted to document his fishing trips with some photos of his catch. The only problem was that the most photogenic big fish catches had been hauled in by some other angler. So, he established the habit of having his photo taken with someone else's fish. He would just walk up to someone and ask if he could have his picture taken with the fish. Of course, this was the person who had actually caught the fish.

Dad, with someone else's fish

    He never really claimed to have caught the fish, although for a time he had inferred it until it became widely known the fish were not his. He had quite a photo collection of him holding a fish with a stranger by his side nervously looking on.

    Back in the mid-1950s, my father was working as an accounting clerk for the Postal Service at the main post office in San Francisco. One afternoon he called home. One thing you have to know about my dad is **he never called home,** as in his book personal phone calls would be a waste of taxpayers' money, and his point of view was that he could say all he needed to say when he was at home, so why would he ever call home while working? This day was an exception because he said that he was going to be on the Six O'clock News and we should call all our relatives to let them know. If the phrase, "Must See TV" had been in use then, my father would have said his appearance on TV would have qualified as "Must See TV." Because he did not tell us why he was on the Six O'clock

News, our first reaction is he did something very embarrassing and it would be magnified by his appearance on TV.

He arrived home about 5:00 and he was like the kid in the candy store as he arranged chairs in the living room around our black and white set. He finally revealed that the reason for his appearance on the news was because he had been the victim of an armed robbery by a robber who had mistaken the bank bag my father was carrying as containing cash, when in fact it contained worthless money order receipts. Apparently, the robber had noticed my father regularly carried this bank bag from the post office to a downtown bank. Before he could provide us with any more details, the Six O'clock News came on channel 5. The lead reporter was Fort Pearson, a veteran newspaperman who was doing the news on TV. Back in those days, most television reporters were real newsmen and not TV personalities who mainly just read the news. Pearson had black hair slicked back on his head, and he had a pencil thin mustache that made him look like Dick Tracy of the comics. There was no happy talk chit chat in those days, it was serious news reporting. My father's robbery was the lead story on KPIX that night, and Pearson introduced it by reporting that a postal clerk faced off an armed robber in downtown San Francisco today and the postal clerk was in the studio for his first-hand account. Pearson had managed just one question when my dad grabbed the microphone out of the hand of the startled newscaster.

I must say my dad looked pretty distinguished on the tube as the cameraman zoomed in on him for a close-up. My dad now had the microphone, and he was not going to give it up as he launched into a monologue about the robbery. He was going to squeeze his fifteen minutes of fame into a three-minute soliloquy. He explained that the poor sad robber had picked out a victim who was not carrying any money. He launched into an explanation to the robber of the fact the post office would probably never trust him to carry cash and explained the money order system to the thief. He then went into his personal story that his wife only allowed him to take enough cash each day for his carfare and his lunch. He even told the robber where he ate each day to make the most out of his lunch money. He concluded his monologue by telling the robber that he had five children to support on a postal clerk's salary. At that point in the interview, Fort Pearson had regained control of the microphone and told my father he was happy my dad had not been hurt in the robbery. I thought my dad may have been the first person to have talked a robber into submission.

About ten years later, in 1968, I had graduated from San Francisco State and had been hired by the State of California Department of Employment as an Investigator Trainee. I was living at home and was engaged to be married and the wedding would be in October. Although my parents were happy that I had obtained a job, I think my father was more impressed by the fact that I had been issued a State of California attaché case. In reality, the attaché case was not all that impressive. It was a dull tan color, and rather than leather it was mainly some fake plastic with the words "State of California" embossed on the top.

The San Francisco office had hired two recent college graduates in July as investigator trainees. The other trainee was Bill and he had attended on the GI Bill and had already served a term in the Navy, while I had the draft and a military commitment hanging over my head. Bill was in his late twenties and had lived life a bit, while I was in my early twenties and had worked at the post office while I attended college. Our formal training course was scheduled for a few months in the future. So, to get our feet wet, Bill and I were assigned to visit employers in San Francisco and check payroll records for suspected Unemployment Insurance code violations.

Each morning, Bill and I would be given our audit forms indicating potential violations, and we would head out to separate areas of San Francisco to conduct employer visits. One day, we had returned to the office at the end of the day and Bill looked a bit weary. He came up to my desk and said, "**Guess who I ran into today?**" The weary look and his roll of his eyes told me without a doubt --- he had encountered my father. Just like many adolescents see the presence of their parents around their friends as a situation fraught with embarrassment, that is how I felt about Bill encountering my father. Bill just smiled and shook his head. "Your dad is a real piece of work." I meekly replied, "Yes he is." Bill said he was standing on a busy street corner in downtown San Francisco waiting for the light to change when a man came up beside him. The man glanced at Bill's State of

California attaché case and casually asked, "**Do you work with my kid?**" Of course, with a few thousand state employees working in San Francisco among the 800,000 residents, no way could my father have encountered a man I did actually work with.

Bill reported that my father's close-talking technique had cornered him against a pole as my dad launched into a 20-minute monolog about me giving up the comforts of my room at home and my mom's cooking to get married. This became one of my dad's bits one I had become engaged. It could be kind of funny when he did it with my friends and family, but here he was sharing it with a relative stranger of mine.

All Bill could say was, "**You know, your dad is a real character.**"

Poppy, my dad
Mission High School Graduation
San Francisco, 1923

WHEN DID YOU LAST SEE YOUR FATHER?

The movie "When Did You Last See Your Father?" struck a chord with me when I saw it a few years ago. The film is the true story of an adult son, British writer Blake Morrison, attending to the dying days of his father. Its message is an elegy to a father and a tribute to the unending efforts of children to comprehend their receding childhood. Somehow, this film captured a feeling of a son who was both enthralled and exasperated by his father, who was complex and difficult for his son to comprehend both in life and near his death. It was something I had dealt with in trying to comprehend my father and my relationship with him. I had to find the book that the movie was based upon.

When Did You Last See Your Father? is the book's title and the title of the final chapter where Blake Morrison wrote in the opening of the chapter:

"**When did you last see your father?**" *Was it when they burnt the coffin? Put the lid on? When he exhaled his last breath? When he last sat up and said something? When he last recognized me? When he last smiled? When he last did something for himself unaided? When he last felt healthy? When he last thought he might be healthy before they brought him the news? I keep trying to find that last moment when he was still unmistakably there, in the fullness of his being him.*

"**When did you last see your father?**" *Maybe it was my own father who had used the phrase. I remember him telling me, at some point in my late teens or twenties when I was drifting away from him, seeing less of him, how badly he had taken the death of his father, and how he did not want it to happen to me. "I used to see Grandpa every weekend. But for some reason, I'd not seen him for about six weeks, and then he had his heart attack and then he was dead. There had been some rows between us that we had not* *settled. I recall someone at the wake asking, 'When did you last see your father?' And me feeling just terrible."*

I interrogate myself: **When did you last see your father?** *I wanted to warn people not to underestimate filial grief; don't think that just because you no longer live with them or have had a difficult relationship with them or are grown and perhaps are a parent yourself, don't think it will make it any easier when they die. I used to think the world is divided between those who have children and those who don't; now I think it is divided between those who've lost a parent and those whose parents are still alive.*

In writing about my father, I hear his voice in my head. You fathead. Seventy-five bloody years I lived, over forty years while you were alive yourself, and all you get is me looking like death warmed over. You daft sod – do you think dying is anything to write home about, is that any sort of story? Let's hear about some of the good times, the holidays, the golf and the tennis. What is such a big deal about death? No, tell them about all the fun we had and the things we built – write about life.

Back in London, the therapist asks, 'How long has it been since he died. **When did you last see your father?"***

I remember the answer then, and I tell her."

When had I last seen my own father? I think back to January of 1981 when I was summoned by my brother to come from Sacramento to San Francisco to give my mother a break for the weekend from caring for my bedridden father. My father had been diagnosed with terminal cancer before he had even informed us of his situation the prior year. It was so typical of him not to inform us that he was dying in order to keep everything the same. Although he liked being the center of attention with his jokes or stories or as we referred to them, his "Poppy routines," his health was something that he would want to keep private and hidden, even from his family, or maybe especially from his family.

He had been bedridden at home for months, as my entire family, my mother, three sisters, and brother were in agreement that his final days would be spent in the family home on 19th Avenue where my parents had lived for over fifty years. Both of my parents were in their mid-seventies and caring for my father had taken its toll on my mother both physically and emotionally.

The man I saw in that bed was my father, but not my father. He was shrunken and shriveled, a shell of the six-foot-tall, robust man he been most of my life. The man with a twinkle in his eye and a story or routine on his lips, a man who would start most of his stories with "wait until you hear this one, this is the best one yet," the person in the bed was a shell of that person. Not only was his physical presence altered but also missing was his spirit, and I thought, **When did I last see my father?**

I was in my mid-thirties, and this was the closest and most personal encounter I'd had with death, and I was scared for my father and for myself. I thought about what I needed to say and what I needed to do, and I suddenly realized that of the many family, fatherly and personal situations in the past when I did not know what to do, I would usually call my father to ask his opinion or seek his counsel. I admit I did not always agree with his ideas, opinions, solutions or viewpoints, but he was always there to listen to me, offer ideas and suggestions based on his own experiences. He always reassured me that whatever the outcome or whatever course of action I took, things would usually work out, and I thought **When did I last see my father?**

I kept the vigil at Dad's bedside. For the most part, he was unaware of my presence. As I helped him turn over, he looked at me and said. "Take it easy, Jim." These were the last words he would speak to me. He spent the rest of the day sleeping or slipping in and out of consciousness. Occasionally, he would startle me by talking in his slumber. He would call out to his friends back in the Mission District, going back decades in his mind, "Come on, Ed we are meeting the guys down at 18th and Capp." Or he would talk about a ball game that was forming up at the schoolyard. I felt like an intruder into this part of his life. I wondered, was his life flashing by in his mind? It was not for me to fathom the workings of his mind at the time that his death was imminent.

And as I left him quietly sleeping in his room, I thought back to when was that time when I last saw my father most fully being himself and the person he was when he was most alive. Later that evening my father passed from this world, and amid all the sadness I thought to myself, When did I last see my father when he was most fully himself? I smiled when I recalled my "last fling trip" with him to Mendocino before I was married in 1968.

RUNNING IN MY FAMILY

I have always loved running. It was an activity that seemed so natural to me as far back as I can remember. It was something I could do by myself, under my own power, and that I could do fast or slow, and it was almost as natural as breathing. When I was a young boy in San Francisco, in elementary school it was racing with my friends to the corner store or across the street, or around the block down to the park. It seems like we were always running and racing. I found out that I was pretty fast, and I realized later that it was part of me that likely had come down from my ancestors.

My brother was four years older than me, and he had achieved some success and recognition through his running. At St. Cecilia's School, he was the fastest boy in the entire school; he would go on to be a record-setting distance runner in high school, and ultimately, he received a track scholarship to the University of New Mexico. When I followed him in high school, I too ran track and cross-country. Even though I achieved some success and won some races, I don't think it was the competition with others that motivated me to run. It was just the act of running and how it made me feel that kept me running in the days before it was trendy or known as a beneficial form of exercise. It was something I could do for myself, on my own. When I ran I felt free, alone with my thoughts in a sort of stream of consciousness form of meditation. I just always felt better when I ran.

From miles to marathons, it became a lifestyle, a form of positive addiction that I did for decades without really understanding exactly why except that it was an activity I had to do make myself complete. I know there are people who love to run and people who hate it. It can be painful or it can be exhilarating; it can be meaningful or meaningless, all on the same run. It was an itch that I regularly had to scratch. I learned a lot about my heart, mind and will by running, especially the marathons I ran which were some of the greatest challenges of my life both physically and mentally. At around twenty miles your body and mind cry **Stop! Stop! It hurts! It's painful!** But somehow, I managed running through that mythical wall at twenty miles to finish the twenty-six point-two-mile run.

I have learned over the years that running is definitely in the genes of the Mullany family. When researching the Mullany family history, I learned that in the 1920s the family regularly attended the coal dealers' association picnics that always included foot races. In a letter from that time, my father wrote, *"The committee put up a squawk that I was entered in the married men's race – the fifty-yard dash. I was a runner with a bunch of five milers, as I was fifteen yards ahead at the twenty-five-yard mark. I was tempted to go the last ten yards on my hands and knees. The others did so poorly I believe because they were boozing all day."* The Mullany brothers dominated the foot races year after year at the picnic. The boys would always make a haul of all the prizes. Even my mother seemed to have that talent, as in 1925 she won the single woman's race and won six silver spoons as a prize.

The running bug even extended to my daughters. When my youngest daughter Adrienne entered high school, she was encouraged to participate in extracurricular activities. On her own, with little encouragement from her parents, she settled on track and cross-country running and stuck with those activities for the entire four years of high school. Although she may not have collected wins and medals, her participation enabled her to meet a group of kids who became like a family of friends to her in high school. She did her miles and miles and formed the foundation for a healthy lifestyle that endures to this day. She now regularly goes out for runs at 5:00 am to carve out the time to run as a busy mother of two, running in her San Jose neighborhood. Her 5:00 am runs are something of déjà vu moments for me, as I did the same routine in our Pacifica neighborhood back in the 1970s when my daughters were young.

My older daughter Erin has become a regular runner too, in order to help her participate in triathlons and also help to deal with the stress and strain of being a working mother with a child under two years old. I am particularly proud of the fact that she has created a stronger bond with her husband, who a few years ago, claimed he was not a runner and never would be one. Now he too is a regular runner, participating in runs and races and training for triathlons. It was especially heartwarming for me to see him heading out for a run with the jogging stroller and grandson Ian James along for the run. Running has literally has run through our family for generations, and those bonds running has created are some of the strongest in the family. And almost a century after my father and mother won those races at the coal dealers' picnic, my three-year-old grandson Cameron recently proclaimed to me, "You know Poppa, I can run really fast!" I know Cameron, I know.

My Two Families

The following two essays are about my two families — the family of my birth and my married family. Although the two families had some connections, as a man and a son those connections were complicated. I hope these two essays do justice to both families.

My Birth Family

I was born in San Francisco in February 1945. I was the youngest of five children: my oldest sister, Ann was eleven years older than me, sister Maureen (Moe) was ten years older than me, sister Lou was eight years older than me, and brother Mike was four years older than me. The family was Irish-Catholic as were many of our neighbors in the Parkside District of San Francisco. There were also many Italian families and others of European origins.

One thing I want to make perfectly clear from the start, **I was NOT a Baby Boomer**. That designation applies to children who were born after the end of World War II from about 1947 until the mid-1950s. It generally applies to men who returned home at the end of the War to have children with their wives who were at home during the War. I am not a baby boomer because I was born before the end of the War, and coincidentally my father was a postal clerk who was not a member of the armed services. It has been something of pet peeve of mine to be lumped into the group called Baby Boomers because I was not a baby boomer by any definition. In fact, as far as I know there was no cute name designation for those of us who were born during the war. Those Americans who served during the War or who were adults during this period have been called The Greatest Generation for their role in helping to win the War.

Depending upon which member of the family is telling the story, you likely will have five significantly different versions of our family. The birth order, the ages, the sexes and the era in which we matured all had an influence on the family history you might hear. My sisters were all born in the 1930s and were raised during the War Years of the 1940s, while my brother Mike was a young boy in the 1940s. I have always viewed myself primarily as kid of the 1950s, even though most of my high school and college years were in the 1960s.

I loved growing up in the 1950s, it was a time of safety and security with the great freedom we had. If you ask any person who grew up in the 1950s, you likely will hear that parents always wanted kids to be outside playing and not hanging around the house watching television. In fact, many mothers of that era sent us kids outside in the mornings and ordered us not to return until the streetlights came on. When kids were outside, we had minimal contact or supervision by our parents or any adults. It was up to us to find things to do and places to go. I might call us the "autonomous generation" – we loved being kids on our own. My sisters said they were granted the same freedoms to be outside and on their own as boys were.

To modern parents, this type of parenting might sound neglectful or dangerous for children, but to most children during those times there were few if any dangers associated with being a child. We organized our own sandlot pickup sports and games without parental involvement or interference and we explored the neighbor or the city on our bikes or riding on the bus. We were given enough loose change for carfare or penny candy, and that was about all we needed. The one thing I recall is we usually resolved our disagreements or problems on our own. In fact, the kid who called mom or dad to resolve a kids' issue was usually derided or ridiculed. The same rules seemed to apply to our siblings too. Parental involvement in organized sports and games was also very minimal. I recall playing CYO (Catholic Youth Organization) baseball and basketball during the 1950s. Our coaches were recreation directors or college age kids.

Some parents (usually stay-at-home moms) might drive us to practice or games, but that was the extent of parental involvement. Childhood back then was for kids, not for adults.

There were two significant events in my early childhood that I have no memory of. The first one was that I was born with severe hip dysplasia, a condition where the top of the leg does not fit properly into the hip socket. The condition is in most instances an inherited condition that occurs in about 1 of every 1,000 births. In my case, I was treated with a Spica cast, which is almost a full body cast with an extension on the leg/hip that has dysplasia. The theory was the leg joint is forced to grow into the hip socket properly. In my case, I was in the cast for over almost two years. I am told that I had to sleep on a bed that was lined with wooden boxes to prevent me from falling out of bed. I was told that I was a pretty pathetic looking infant in the body cast. For me the process did not work, and I have walked with my left leg turned in and with a slight limp my entire life. The limp was most pronounced when I was tired. Fortunately, the condition never caused me pain, nor did arthritis ever develop in the hip. I have always have been able to fully participate in sports and games. The condition did make me subject to tripping, as I have always had a tendency not to lift my left leg up as high as the right one when I walk. I loved sports and I ran long distances and played sports most of my life. I never knew if the condition had an impact on my performance in sports. A somewhat psychological impact the condition has had on me is I have been sensitive to the fact people sometimes point out "my limp." My friends and relatives became used to me walking the way I do, but others have regularly asked throughout my life, "Did you hurt your leg?" Or, "**What is wrong with your leg?**" As a shy kid and an introverted adult, this attention has at times angered me, even though most people who brought it up meant well. To varying degrees, some of the children of my sister Ann and my own two daughters had the condition.

The second event that I have no memory of happened when I was a baby in the cast. There are some different versions of this story in my family. My older brother Mike was playing with matches under the inside staircase in our home and he caught the house on fire. The fire necessitated the fire department coming to our house to extinguish the blaze. It was a Sunday morning and my mother was out – she was either at church or at the store – and my father was also gone at the time, so it is believed that one of my sisters was home. My mother arrived back home to see the fire trucks and firemen at our house, and she screamed, **"Where's Jimmy?"** The firemen were not aware that I was upstairs sleeping. The controversy or conflict of the incident was a question that has never been answered. Was Mike was trying to burn down the house with me in it because he was jealous of the attention I was receiving, or was he just playing with matches and accidentally started the fire? Mike's motives have never been determined as he was only five or six years old at the time. A joke later told about the story is that Mike's response to my mother's question was, **"Who is Jimmy?"** In a bit of irony, later in life Mike became a San Francisco Fireman.

  I loved being a child and growing up in the 1950s in San Francisco. The City, as everyone called it then, was a city of districts, parishes and neighborhoods. The world was familiar with the landmarks, bridges, hills, and the views and landscapes of the ocean and the City by The Bay. To those who lived in the city, our world was one of neighborhoods, districts or parishes. My world happened to be the Parkside neighborhood in the Sunset District and St. Cecilia's Parish. Except for trips downtown for shopping or excursions across one of the bridges, our life was centered upon and fully experienced in our district and parish. In the 1950s, families living in the Parkside planned to live their entire lives there – moving up to better homes and neighborhoods was just not much of a consideration. So, you would know the neighborhood families, kids and merchants your entire life. For example, throughout my attendance at St. Cecilia's grammar school, I attended school pretty much with the same group of classmates from kindergarten through the 8th grade and with some boys all the way through high school. This same constancy applied to our neighbors on 19th Avenue.

  We were fortunate in that much of the recreation of the city was a short bus or street car ride away, from the beach to the zoo to Playland at the Beach to Golden Gate Park and its many recreational opportunities. By the fourth or fifth grade, most kids in San Francisco knew the bus routes sufficiently to travel around the city on their own or with friends. Many adults also used public transportation to get them to work, school or shopping as most families in the City had just one car. I was fortunate to live directly across the street from Larsen Park, which had ball fields, a playground, basketball and tennis courts. From a very young age, it was my second home. Also, I lived right around the corner from St. Cecilia's grammar school and its school yard. For me, my Parkside neighborhood was "kid Nirvana." There was always a group of boys my age to play sports and games with. Because I was a shy kid, the language of my communication was sports – I always felt that I belonged when I was playing sports

As a child, I felt that I belonged to two separate families. First, there were my parents and my older sisters; they all seemed like adults to me when I was a child. The main thing I recall about my sisters, who were twelve, ten and eight years older than me, was that they were more caretakers and babysitters. I have a special memory of each one of them taking me on outings. With Ann, it was in 1955 when she took me to a USF basketball game at the Cow Palace in San Francisco. The University of San Francisco was the best college basketball team in the nation then and it was so exciting for me to see some of their games. With sister Maureen, I recall her taking me to a San Francisco Seals baseball game at Seals Stadium and how I insisted that we had to stay until the end of the game, as I insisted "the game was never over until the last out was made." For Lou, it was an outing to downtown San Francisco and how Lou had us on the wrong streetcar line and we had no money for another car and how we had to walk about five miles over Twin Peaks in the pouring rain. We were both drenched, but all I recall of the incident was how Lou was berated by Mother for getting "little Jimmy all wet." I did not know my sisters very well as girls due to our age differences and I felt that I only really got to know them as adults.

I was the shy, quiet member of a very outgoing and talkative family. Ours was something of the typical, large Irish Catholic family of the time – lots of kids and everyone talking at once; trying to be heard was a matter of talking louder than the other kids, as seldom was there much listening going on. In this environment, as the baby of a family of world class talkers the battles for dominance had already been won well before I was ever born. I preferred to be the invisible one in this group; to be noticed was not always a good thing for me. So, I worked at being invisible, although in our family I did not really have to work all that hard to be invisible as the others tended to ignore me.

As I got older, whenever I was home I would usually quietly disappear unnoticed into my bedroom to listen to baseball or basketball games on the radio or to read. As I got older, I figured out how to keep scorecards in baseball and basketball and would spend many hours listening to ball games and filling up scorebooks. Something about my solitary nature and trying to make order out of life made scorekeeping a natural fit for me. I was invisible and happy about it because I did not have much to contribute to the family conversations, nor did I feel I was ever really missed by the rest of the family. Over time, my father became my ally in my solitary pursuits, as he would either tape record games I would miss or he would fill out my scorecards on his own. This required him to listen to hours and hours of games on the radio. He somehow enjoyed it as much as I did. The most memorable time was when he kept score for me in the longest major league game in history – a twenty-three inning game between the Giants and the Mets. It lasted over six hours. So, he may not have said he loved me, but he demonstrated it with the time he spent on me.

Then there was the rest of my family. My brother Mike, I think he went well-beyond the typical mean and cruel older brother. He was literally "THE star of the family," especially to my mother. He was the star in sports: he excelled in most sports he tried, especially those which had running as their foundation. I was four years younger than him and quiet, so I literally and figuratively grew up in his shadow for much of my young life. He was for a time the fastest runner in St. Cecilia's elementary school's student body and also was a standout baseball player. In high school, he chose to concentrate on track and cross country as his sports because in those sports, as he said, "he did not have to share the recognition or glory with any teammates." He excelled in those sports and held school distance running records for many years, and later he was inducted into the Riordan High School Hall of Fame. (More about Mike in the Essay, *My Brother, Mike*)

Like many Irish-American families of the post-World War II period, we were not very demonstrative or touchy-feely about expressing our feelings. I cannot recall my parents ever telling me that they loved me and they definitely were not huggers and kissers. I can recall that few of the Irish-Catholic families I knew during this time were demonstrative of their feeling. Most fathers went to work and brought home the money to put food on the table and a roof over our heads, and that was how the men expressed their love of family in those days, and stay-at-home moms of a large family expressed their love by doing the cooking, cleaning, shopping and caring for the kids. I think we felt or assumed that we were loved, but on the other hand, we grew up realizing that the world did not revolve around us kids.

When all of my older sisters had moved out of the house and my brother had started college at Monterey Peninsula College in 1959, I suddenly felt I had been transformed from the invisible youngest child of a family of five kids, to an only child in a quiet house where I would get the undivided attention of my parents. Unfortunately, I had not factored the impact the addition of grandchildren would have upon our household. My oldest sister Ann, as a traditional Catholic wife, started to literally and figuratively "reproduce" the accomplishment of her mother by having children. In the end, she would match my mother by having five children of her own. The impact on me was that while I was still in the home at thirteen years old, my parents, most particularly my mother, transformed into being full-time grandparents and at times forgot about their child at home. My mother started to regularly spend entire days with my sister Ann, helping out with the grandkids or else we would have them at our house. High chairs, portable playpens, diapers and baby clothes took over our house. As a grandparent myself now, I understand that grandkids can be more fun and exciting than caring for your own children.

I later would identify this as a specific period that I grew apart from my mother and grew closer to my father. He was around the house more than my mom and was more available for me to talk to than my mother was. Also, the issues I started facing at that time in my life were best suited to be discussed with my dad than with my mom. College, my future career, getting a car, getting a job, the draft, my brother Mike, were topics I could talk about with my dad rather than with my mother. My mother was a telephone person and spent endless hours talking on the phone to her mother and my sisters, so she was more often mentally and physically away from our house. Also, when I was in high school, I think I became fully aware how she favored my brother Mike over me. I would overhear conversations where she would be talking about things Mike had done or said. For her, I think that it came down to Mike had a personality that was funny and the life of the party while I was the quiet one who did well in school and never gave my parents any problems, I somehow lacked that personality that she so valued.

In high school, I had some modest success in basketball and track where I won a few races here and there, but I never came close to matching my brother's glory. I believe I had something of a self-esteem issue due to comparisons to my brother. My friends kidded me about how I had to walk into the gymnasium every day and look up to the "wall of fame" where my brother's school records were posted. That part of it did not bother me much in school as it was sometimes neat to be recognized, even if it was just for being the brother of the school record holder. But in my senior year, in a small way I established my own identify at Riordan. I had worked hard in the summer training for the fall cross-country season. It paid off, as I started regularly to win or come close to winning in our cross-country races in Golden Gate Park. At Riordan they had a tradition of ringing a "victory bell" in the main hallway to announce team or individual victories. In addition, whenever the victory bell rang, the school's public-address system made an announcement as to why the victory bell was being rung. In the fall of 1958, a number of times the victory bell was rung to announce a cross-country team victory in which my name was announced as the individual winner. It was neat to have my name announced, but what was really great was there was never a comparison or mention of my brother, as most of the classmates who knew of my brother's glory had already graduated and were no longer around.

At the fall sports award ceremony, I was recognized as the Most Valuable Runner on the Cross-Country Team at Riordan. It was the first time in my life that I had received an individual recognition award. I had been on many championship baseball and basketball teams at St. Cecilia's school, but every award I received was a team award. Also, back in those days there were no such things as trophies for participation; the trophies and awards had to be won or earned. Although it did not come close to the awards and recognition my brother had received, the award was mine and mine alone. I came home that day with the trophy with my name engraved on it, along with a certificate with a description of what I had accomplished to win the award. I remember placing it on a table so my parents would see it, but I did not say anything about it. My dad saw it and might have said something like congratulations and that was about it. I do not recall if my mother saw it, but I do remember that neither parent said they were proud of me, nor do I think they ever told anyone else in the family. It stung and stayed with me a long time, considering all the glory and recognition Mike had received in the family. I guess I thought it was because I just did not have that personality.

In the early 1960s when I attended high school, my family had radically changed, in that my four older siblings no longer lived at home in San Francisco. I in essence had become an only child after having spent my entire life as the youngest or baby of the family. Coinciding with this change in our household, my oldest sister Ann had married and started her own family in the late 1950s when she had her first child, Suzanne, and in fairly rapid succession she had four boys. My mother also was transformed from Mom to Nana as she put the majority of her time and attention to being a grandmother. This meant towards the end of my high school years, my primary relationship in the family was with my father. He also was starting to focus on his role as Poppy, as he loved to have outings with his grand kids. I was fine with this new family dynamics because like many teenagers, I was pretty much self-absorbed with my own activities. Also, I had some fun with the grand kids who had started to supplant my older siblings as regular visitors at our home. And, it was nice to pick up some spending money by babysitting my niece and nephews.

    I don't think I have ever been one of those children to blame my problems or personal issues on my parents or on the way I was raised, as I think my parents were pretty fair and did their best to provide a safe and secure home to their children. I came to realize that my parents, especially my mother, seem to rank the kids in the family and my brother demanded and received much attention from my parents. He was a talented athlete and a life-of-the-party type who very selfishly craved attention. He once told me that he and my father competed for center stage in the family and outside of the home. He craved and demanded attention. I have a separate essay about my brother Mike in this collection of essays. I was happy when he went away to college as he could be mean and cruel to me, especially when he was showing off to his friends and made me the target of his jokes. Also, he could be moody.

    With my mother focusing on her grandkids, my connection to my father became closer as I neared graduation from high school in the early 1960s. My father was not much of an advocate for having his children attend college. I think he pretty much left that decision up to us. I recall a discussion I had with him about college that led him giving me a talk on "the facts of life" – the economic or financial facts of life. I had no real plan with regard to attending college other than thinking I would follow the lead of my friends who were planning to attend Catholic Colleges in Northern California. The popular choices were the University of San Francisco, St. Mary's University and Santa Clara University. I did not realize that all of these schools had high admission standards and very high tuition rates, or that my friends would have been covered by their parents. My father told me that if I planned on going to college, I would have to find a way to pay the tuition and fees. He said that when my brother's scholarship at the University of New Mexico was cut, he (my father) was left holding the bag for the final year's tuition. He informed me that he would not be paying for my college education. I had no real plan for college with regard to what I would take, where I would go and how I would pay for it.

My father told me that a good possibility for a job would be at the post office at Rincon Annex in San Francisco. You had to be eighteen years old to be hired, but one could take the written test at seventeen years old. The postal service had a jobs program that was geared to students. I took the examination and was hired in the spring of 1963 when I was still in high school. The job was five days a week, four hours a night, and the position included pay that was twice the minimum wage and included vacation and sick leave benefits along with medical insurance.

Little did I know this job would change my life forever in ways I could have never anticipated. Before graduation, I had anticipated completing my track season while I worked. For about two months, my schedule was I went to track practice at 6:00 am, then did a full day of high school until 3:00 pm, and I then took the streetcar to work from 5:00 pm until 9:00 pm. I arrived home close to 10:00 pm – exhausted. Sadly, I was not strong enough to maintain this schedule and compete in track meets at my best. I was disappointed when, because of fatigue from my schedule, I did not do well at the league meet running the mile run – I was disappointed not to qualify for the district meet. My track career was over, but my life was beginning.

In the fall of 1963 I enrolled at San Francisco State College and I continued to live at home and work part time for the post service. My dad told I would have to pay room and board to my mother for the work in the house she did for me. I would have to pay her about $100 a month.

The schedule at college and working at the post office was perfect for a college student because during the Christmas and summer periods there were opportunities for me to work overtime and earn extra money. I was able to buy a car and set up a bank account. Back in those days, there were no ATM machines or quick ways to get cash, so I had to keep an envelope of cash in the drawer in my bedroom. At some point in my work life the post office, my mother started to take cash from the envelope and leave me IOU notes. She would not ask me in person, she would just go into the envelope, take cash without asking and leave me a note. I recall once when she left me with zero cash and I had planned to attend a Giants game that weekend and had no access to cash I was angry but became livid when I learned my mother needed the money to buy something for the grandkids. Neither of us knew at this time, but another woman would soon be coming into my life.

The Mullany Family - 1957

July 15 at Moe's Birthday Party
Lake Tahoe
Mike (74), Ann (82), Moe (80), Jim (70), Lou (78)

My Married Family

After about two years at the post office, I met Bonnie and my life was transformed. Bonnie was nineteen years old, a City College Student, and I was twenty-one years old, and after a period of dating we came to presume that we would be married. My father joked that we got to "play post office" while working at the post office.

I guess our relationship became pretty obvious when one day a mail handler friend named "Shep" smiled and said to me, "**I do believe that James is in love.**" Our job assignments of working the cancellation or stacking machines or sorting magazine flats provided us many opportunities to work together and to get to know each other.

Bonnie had four sisters and a little brother and lived with her mother, who had been divorced a couple of times. As Bonnie's older sister Judy was married and not living at home, Bonnie had assumed many of the maternal duties at home. Bonnie looked very young with ribbons in her hair, but she had many responsibilities at home that had made her grow up fast. As I got to know and became part of Bonnie's family, my role totally changed from what it was in my own family. I was like the older brother in to Bonnie's three younger sisters and her baby brother. I think her mother adored me and she was always providing with me snacks and goodies whenever I visited. I really enjoyed my new role in this family as much more than "the role of the quiet one" or the invisible little brother in my own family. I felt that my individuality started to emerge during the years Bonnie and I were dating.

Bonnie was (and is) one of the smartest people I had ever known. She is smart on every level – academically a well-rounded, complete student in all subjects with common sense and practical smarts – if she did not know something, she would usually figure it out. And she has great people skills – she knows how to communicate with all types of people. Working with Bonnie, I saw how well she worked and communicated with people at the post office. She had confidence in that if she did not know how to do something she believed she could learn how to do it. I worried a bit about how she would get along with my family, and most especially my parents. My dad and Bonnie got along great, and they enjoyed matching wits with each other with verbal jousting. My dad loved to shock people with some of his "giving them the business." He enjoyed the fact Bonnie always had verbal comebacks to him.

My mother was a different matter. Although she and Bonnie were cordial and I don't think there was any of the mother-in-law "she is not good enough for my son," I think even from the start my mother, who was a staunch Catholic, had expected I would meet and marry another Catholic. Although my mother never mentioned it outright, I think the fact Bonnie's mom had been married a couple of times and the fact Bonnie was a strong and somewhat outspoken young woman may have rubbed against the image my mother had of what a young wife should be. None of this was spoken, but it was felt. My sisters Ann, Maureen and Lucille seemed to be the ideal for my mother. Bonnie was just different from them. Also, my brother Mike had married a beautiful, glamorous German girl, Ute, while he was serving in Germany, although Ute was not a Catholic and had a young son when she married my brother. My parents adored Ute, who was apparently all they desired in a daughter-in-law. Ute was kind and gracious to my parents, and they adored her.

Bonnie and I were married in October of 1968 and we resided near both of our families when we moved into our first apartment in Daly City. I definitely felt like I was more of a member of Bonnie's family than my own, but I think that a man becoming part of his wife's family is rather typical.

I started working with the State of California Department of Employment a few months before we were married, and I knew that it was inevitable that I would be drafted into the military service. Instead of being drafted into the Army, I signed up for a four-year enlistment in the Air Force. The four years we lived away from our families was an important period in cementing our own identity and independence. This was especially true when our first child, Erin, was born in January 1973 at March Air Force Base in Riverside, California, although the addition of a new grandchild in the family was an important time for our parents too.

Upon my discharge from the Air Force, we returned to the San Francisco Bay Area to live in first Daly City and later Pacifica, where we had a second addition to our family when Adrienne was born in July 1976. We both loved San Francisco and Pacifica. I think we were sure that we would spend the rest of our lives living in the suburbs of San Francisco.

We were saddened by the fact that my sister Ann, her husband, and the five Regan kids were transferred to Wichita, Kansas. Bonnie and I were closest to the Regan family, although my brother Mike and sister-in-law Ute had been very good to Bonnie while I was in basic training in Texas and Bonnie remained at home. During this time, Ute and Bonnie became closer friends.

Of course, once we were positive that we would remain in the San Francisco Bay Area, we ended up moving to the Sacramento area. When a promotion opportunity arose for me with the State, we realized it was too good to pass up. The State would pay for us to relocate, we would have a temporary housing relocation allowance and a healthy pay raise. But beyond those incentives, the cost of living and housing were much more reasonable in Sacramento, and with Erin ready to start kindergarten we believed the educational system and opportunities would be better for our girls. Also, there was a slight bonus – we felt that putting a bit of distance from our families might be better for us in order to establish our independence. An added bonus that came up later was that Sacramento State University had an excellent accounting program that afforded Bonnie the opportunity to get a degree in accounting that later led her to becoming a Certified Public Accountant.

But one problem with my original family, and most particularly my mother, persisted – my relative standing in her rating of the family hierarchy. Although she was thrilled with the addition of more grandchildren, the status of my brother, Ute and his family soared. Nana, as she was known to the family as a grandmother, just loved Ute and Mike's family in a special way. Once we moved to the Sacramento area, there became a distinct pattern to our visits to my parents. My father always wanted to take me and the girls to an outing to the beach or parks, as he said he wanted to "get away from the women's talk." But this left Bonnie in an uncomfortable position of spending uneasy hours with my mother while my dad and I had fun outings with the girls. I was surprised the first time Bonnie told me that my mother went into a mean and cruel attack mode when she was alone with Bonnie. Bonnie said she was not sure where it came from – was it a personality clash, or the fact of Bonnie's non-Catholic background, or the fact that Bonnie was younger, or the fact we as a family paled in comparison to Mike and Ute? All were possibilities.

I did not know what to do, so I did nothing. It finally came to a head when Bonnie informed me that she could no longer handle these sessions with my mother and future visits with the girls to Nana and Poppy in San Francisco would have to be my responsibility. It clearly was a serious problem, as it had gotten to the point it was having an impact on our relationship.

My daughter Erin adored her Nana from the start and loved to spend time with her and talk with her on the phone. Erin liked shopping with Nana and visiting at Nana and Poppy's house in San Francisco and she loved outings in San Francisco. But this relationship changed when Erin realized although Nana was good to her when she and her sister Adrienne were alone visiting with Nana (after Poppy had passed away), it was different when other cousins were also visiting. Erin felt a few times she was not wanted around Nana's house at those times, and even the Regan boys had noticed that difference. It hit Erin very hard when she realized that her mom was not being treated too well by Nana. At a certain point, Erin mentioned that she felt Nana did not like her and it was extremely painful to her. Erin was about nine years old when she came to this realization. How does a parent deal with something like this? In my case, I tried to make excuses or come up with explanations to Erin, but once again I really did nothing. I felt if I had confronted my mother, she would go into her denial mode. What could I do – say to my mother that if it came down to my mother or my wife and child, it was ultimately going to be mother who would lose us? It was a hard, no-win situation in my mind, so I continued to do nothing, and to this day I regret it.

  The ultimate exclamation point to the situation, especially as it concerned my children and their Nana, was a discovery I made when visiting our family home after my dad had passed away in the mid 1980's. When I was living in Sacramento, I would regularly come to San Francisco for 49ers games and would sometimes stay overnight at my parents' home. One time near Christmas, I stayed while my mother was visiting with one of my sisters in Santa Rosa. I saw an envelope propped up on the shelf in the breakfast room. My had written a list with the amount of money she would be giving each grandchild for Christmas. The list started with about $50 for the oldest grandchildren down to $20 for the Devine grandchildren, who were about the same ages as my daughters. Down at the very bottom of the list were the names my two daughters Erin and Adrienne with the amount $5 next to each of their names. I was stunned, hurt, and angry, as in my mind I thought this was the worth my children were being given by their grandmother. No matter whatever sense or logic I tried to make out of this list, I came the same conclusion. My children were being rated or ranked based upon Bonnie and me. My question until this day is Why? I never asked my mother, nor did she ever volunteer an explanation.

  I concluded from this experience that in my life as a parent or grandparent, I would never rate or rank my children or grandchildren and would always try to treat them as individuals, but never favor one over the other.

  I learned through marriage and parenthood that there is to a degree a level of dysfunction in all families, because families are composed of people, and people make mistakes or most likely will come into conflict when living as a family group. The outwardly appearing "perfect family" may be hiding a budding mass murderer or serial killer, or at least people or a person hiding a psychological problem or addiction condition. It just goes with being human beings, we want to generally put our best face or family picture forward.

Our family ending up having a nice family life in Sacramento, which seemed to be better suited for raising a family than the San Francisco of the 1970s, 80s and 90s did. Erin and Adrienne received solid educations in the San Juan Unified School District and later with the community college system at Sierra College and Sacramento State University and UC Davis. Bonnie and I were pleased with the way our girls turned out, and as different as they were, I would like to think neither of us played favorites with our daughters. I believe Bonnie was a great mentor and role model for the girls and also advised me on the complexities and subtleties of being a father to teenage girls.

My teaching the girls how to drive was somewhat symbolic of our relationships. Erin and I would come home after a particularly intense session, and the slamming of the doors from the garage would generally herald how well or poorly the lesson had gone, while with Adrienne and me, it was usually an occasion to have breakfast together after the lesson – although years later, I overheard a discussion between Erin and Adrienne about those driving lesson. Apparently, a technique of mine when they drifted toward going out of their lane was me saying, **"You're, drifting! You're drifting!"** Erin asked Adrienne if it used to drive her crazy whenever I cautioned them about drifting. Adrienne replied that it did driver her crazy too. I then interrupted them and said to Adrienne that she never told me it bothered her when I told her she was drifting. Her reply was surprising but informing to me: "Dad, just because I didn't say it didn't mean I wasn't thinking it."

It reminded me of a conversation I heard where my parents were talking about their children. My dad said that whenever he suggested that Mike or Lou do something, they would fight him tooth and nail, yell and scream, but eventually they would come around, while whenever he suggested something to Maureen or me, we would shake our heads in agreement and then go out and do whatever we planned to do in the first place regardless of agreeing with Dad.

Bonnie and I separated in 1995 after twenty-seven years of marriage when the girls were in college and most of child rearing had been completed. There is no good time for a marriage to break up, but all things being considered we had pretty much completed our child rearing phase of our parentage and we believed our daughters had most of the tools they needed to become independent and productive adults. Although there was sadness, grief and disappointment, I don't think there was an abundance of anger at the time. With our daughters' subsequent marriages and parenthood of three wonderful grandchildren, Avery, Cameron and Ian James, I think Bonnie and I have once again become friends, and we are united in our love of our new roles of being Grammy and Poppa.

NOTE: I loved my parents and was eternally grateful for the safety and security they provided, and as my father always said, "you kids never missed a meal and always had a roof over your head." All of this on the salary of a post office accounting clerk. They sacrificed so we all could attend parochial schools and could have a better life than they did. Each of their five kids became a self-sufficient adult and, in my case, as an adult of I have never been out of work. We each had the wonderful childhood experience of growing up in the great City of San Francisco in the 1940s and 1950s.

Adrienne, Bonnie, Erin and Jim
The Mullany family, Citrus Heights, CA

Left to right between the Warriors cheerleaders: Erin and Leo Scarborough, Ian James Scarborough, Cameron Jones, Adrienne Jones, Poppa Jim Mullany, Joel Jones and Avery Jones.

I Left My Heart There

"Don't ever call it Frisco" Herb Caen.
"The City that Knows How ..." William Howard Taft
(He never completed the sentence. It became the motto for the city of San Francisco)

Where I Come From

Many of us wonder about that age-old question, Who am I? For me, the first hint or clue to the answer to that question is San Francisco. I was born and raised in San Francisco, a fourth-generation native on my mother's side tracing some of my roots back to a few years after the Gold Rush. I was born a few months before the end of World War II, so I am neither officially a Baby Boomer nor a member of the "The Greatest Generation," I guess I am a member of the tweener generation.

When I was growing up, almost all of my close relatives either lived in San Francisco or within a fifteen or twenty-mile radius of the City. Yes, that is what we always called it – "the City" with a capital "C", and somehow everyone in the Bay Area knew what you were talking about when you said "The City." The only relative I can recall who lived very far away from the City was Uncle Gerald, who lived in Los Angeles. And of course, we all knew he was weird, strange and eccentric. What other explanation could there be for living in LA, as we usually derisively referred to it? Also, growing up in San Francisco we somehow instinctively knew never, ever to refer to the City as "Frisco," which was an expletive profanity only used by tourists or people from Oakland.

Oakland – now there is another matter. We in San Francisco just had it in our DNA to view the city of Oakland and its inhabitants as inferior to us in every way. My father's only reference to that East Bay City was his warning to everyone he encountered: "Never go east of Oakland," which really meant never go east of Treasure Island on the Bay Bridge – because in his mind Oakland and the east bay were akin to Hell. He always took delight in telling us about a sign that was prominently posted in the tent city in Golden

Gate Park following the 1906 Earthquake and Fire which proclaimed, "Eat, drink and be merry today, for tomorrow you may be sent to Oakland."

Back when I was growing up in San Francisco, if you were asked where you were from, the usual response would be something like North Beach, the Sunset, the Parkside, The Haight, the Mission, the Richmond or some other San Francisco district. For during that era, almost everyone you encountered was another San Franciscan, and your identity was either framed by the district where you lived, or for Catholics like me, it was your church parish that further stamped your identity. The districts of San Francisco were little more than neighborhoods that had evolved or developed their identities by distinctions of their geography, history or the presence of a landmark or distinctive street. As far as I knew, North Beach which was in the northern area of the city but had no identifiable beach, the Mission was the oldest area of the city that had grown up around Mission Dolores, the Richmond had no connection to any "Richmond" that I am aware of, and the "Haight" (spelled H-A-I-G-H-T) would, in the 1960s, ironically be associated with the summer of love and the hippies' fame of the Haight-Ashbury (deriving its name innocently enough from the intersection of Haight and Ashbury Streets).

Although there was some diversity or variation in the population of each district of the City, each seemed to have its own image, identity or stereotype: North Beach was an Italian area; the Richmond was an Asian family area; the Mission was a place generally associated with Latin immigrants from Mexico and South America; The Fillmore and Hunters Point were where black or Negro people resided; and Pacific Heights, St Francis Woods and the Seacliff areas were places reserved for the wealthy families of San Francisco.

The residential area in San Francisco where I was raised was variously called the Sunset, the Avenues, and the Parkside. Its original designation was "The Outside Lands," which it was called back in the 1800s. The area was not even part of San Francisco for years, and at the time of San Francisco's incorporation back in 1850, this area was still considered to be part of Mexico. After many years of legal battles, it actually took an Act of Congress in 1866 to make it part of the City.

To understand where I came from, you must know about the geography and climate of San Francisco. Although, it is a myth that Mark Twain said "the coldest winter I have spent was a summer in San Francisco," it does describe with some accuracy the San Francisco where I come from. San Francisco occupies the tip of a peninsula in Northern California, surrounded on three sides by bodies of water: the Pacific Ocean to the West, the Golden Gate strait to the north and San Francisco Bay to the East. The city of San Francisco is laid out over some forty hills that reach the height of about 1,000 feet, with the east and west sides of the city divided by a series of hills, including Twin Peaks. The hills and the location of San Francisco relative to the bodies of water sometimes causes a variation of temperatures and sky conditions that are dramatically different in the various areas or districts of the city. The most distinctive features of the west side of the city where I am from are wind and fog. A thick fog can roll in off the ocean and cover the entire west side in a matter of minutes. This fog for the west side of San Francisco is most common in the summer. Although the weather forecasts would predict it would clear or lift in the afternoon, on the west side of town more often than not the fog remained throughout the day. But the hills and varying elevations of San Francisco generally meant there would be a complex pattern of fog and sunshine throughout the city.

Back in 1931, a local person wrote of the area where I came from: *There lies a wild, free stretch of desert land between the lashing sea of the Pacific Ocean and the rugged hills. A place where I have loved to go and rest and think of God and sky and sea and the land. A place where I can sink close to earth's bosom and be blessed, a friendly place is gone now before the builder's hand. I want the sand dunes to escape the streets; I want to go where nature's heart still beats.*

Although far less famous than the well-known landmarks and tourist attractions of San Francisco, the place where I come from once was one of the world's largest concentration of ocean-produced sand dunes. The winds, the ocean action of the Pacific and the erosion of the Sierra Nevada Mountain range all contributed to this unique phenomenon. The Parkside District was one of the last developed areas of San Francisco when the construction of housing started in 1905, and one of the main reasons for this was there was a lack of transportation in that area until the streetcar line was completed, linking it to the downtown business districts. An early problem with this area was it was like a wilderness without street lights for many years after homes were built here.

The layout of streets in the area I came from might be called dull, uninspired or boring. The streets running north and south were numbered and called avenues (such as 19th Avenue where I lived) to distinguish them from the numbered "streets" in the eastern area of the city. The numbered avenues ran all the way out to 48th Avenue adjacent to Ocean Beach and the Pacific Ocean. The crossing streets running north and south reflected the names of Spanish and American Indian contributors to California history and were in alphabetical order such as Ortega, Pacheco, Quintara, Rivera, Santiago and the streets of Ulloa and Vicente, which sandwiched our home on 19th Avenue.

Our house on 19th Avenue was built in the 1920s, just when the Parkside District was beginning to be developed as a "suburb" for working-class families. The homes were constructed in an assembly line manner and were sometimes jokingly referred to as "cookie cutter" architectural style – row upon row of nearly identical houses with slightly different facades to distinguish one from the next. Our house was like nearly all the others in our area, in which one was slapped up right next to our neighbors on long narrow lots. Our two-story home had the living space of two bedrooms, one bathroom, a kitchen, living room, and dining room on the upper floor which were connected by a long narrow hallway. The lower or street level had a garage, washroom and storage areas that most people converted into one or two additional bedrooms, for most of the families living in those areas after World War I or World War II had more children than two bedrooms would accommodate. So, one might ask, what made the "cookie cutter" home and neighborhood where I come from so special or unique?

To begin to explain how and why where I come from was special and unique, I must start with my father, James Joseph Mullany and a Danish chicken rancher named Carl Larsen. In my family, my father was always Jim and I was always Jimmy. He was born, raised, and lived his entire life in San Francisco. He was from a time and a generation that spent all of their lives in one neighborhood, one community, and one city. He and my mother bought our family home in San Francisco in 1932 and he remained there until his death in 1981; my mother lived there for another ten years following his death. It was a time when most of our neighbors in the Parkside District remained in the neighborhood for all of their lives.

My father had a passionate love for San Francisco, and it was one of his missions in life to pass along that love and passion to his children. He constantly reminded us of how unique and special our city was and our good fortune to live there. He told us that people came from all over the world to visit San Francisco and see its sights and landmarks. He not only talked about it, he showed us all the wonders and sights that were just out our front door or down the street. Within two or three miles of our home, during a time when kids were free to explore, there was Golden Gate Park with its many attractions for kids; Playland at the Beach with its funhouse, diving bell and amusement rides; Sutro Baths with its seven pools heated to varying temperatures; the Zoo (from which I could hear the roar of lions at night); Fleishhacker Swimming Pool (the largest swimming pool in the United States, which was patrolled by lifeguards in kayaks); Sigmund Stern Grove, an urban forest a few blocks from our house which was noted for its free summer music festivals; and the Pacific Ocean with its dunes and beaches. I recall falling to sleep to the distant tune of fog horns just outside the Golden Gate.

My father not only encouraged us to explore and appreciate these unique attractions of the City, he had a sense of fun and delight in discovering them with us. You see, he was a genuine San Francisco character, a fact that we sensed as kids but really did not fully understand until we were older. That is something we learned from people we would encounter who would tell us with a wink, nod, and rolling of the eyes, that "Your dad is a real character." And it was through the eyes and imagination of a character that we saw and discovered a special San Francisco.

A simple example is a tale he once concocted about an unknown relative of my mothers who had finally secured employment. With great solemnity, he told us how happy and relieved the family was that this lady finally had secured a steady job. He took me and my brother in the car one evening and announced that he had a treat for us; we would be able to observe this relative at work. He then proceeded to take us out to the beach, and with great delight brought us face to face with Laughing Sal, the maniacal mechanical laughing fat lady featured in a window at the Fun House at Playland at the Beach. These types of stories, jokes and little dramas my father concocted were an ongoing part of our discoveries of the unique places and special people of where I come from.

When I think of my father being a genuine San Francisco character, it calls to mind something I read about an unknown street person from Montgomery Street in San Francisco, who addressed the Board of Supervisors in 1890:

> "Gentlemen, as I look over you, I see that anyone
> can become a millionaire, but how many of you
> have the true talent to become a character?"

And about that Danish chicken rancher named Carl Larsen? How did he help to make where I come from unique and special? Carl Larsen came to San Francisco from Denmark in 1869, and he owned a downtown business, the Tivoli Café. In the late 1880s, he began buying up large amounts of land in the wind-swept dunes area in the Outside Lands for Larsen's Chicken Ranch in order to supply his restaurant with eggs and chickens. If there was an incongruity of a chicken ranch located in the foggy, wind-swept dunes, it was not apparent to Mr. Larsen. Mr. Larsen, a lifelong bachelor, was very generous to his adopted home city. He donated large parcels of land to the City for parks and open space. In 1926, Mr. Larsen donated two full city blocks that eventually became Larsen Park, a recreational oasis with a playground, ball fields, basketball and tennis courts, with trees, bushes interspersed throughout. The park eventually included a public swimming pool and a retired Navy fighter jet plane that kids could climb on and explore.

"Larsen," as everyone in the neighborhood called the park, became a recreational wonderland for generations of San Francisco kids. For me, it was quite fortuitously located directly across the street from our home on 19th Avenue. Other than my house and school, more of my childhood was spent in Larsen Park than any other place. From about age seven, when I was able to cross the four lanes of 19th Avenue, until my late teens, Larsen

Park was my second home. The current generation of parents has been referred to as "helicopter parents" for the way they hover around their children, providing constant supervision, security, and involvement at every turn in the lives of their children. For my childhood, it was "You don't think you are going to hang around this house all day underfoot. I don't want to see you back here until it is time for dinner or gets dark" parents. You see this was an era of segregation – kids from adults. Our lives rarely intersected in those days, and I think both groups were grateful for that. My parents had their own version of this divide which went something like, "There is a perfectly beautiful park right across the street, I am sure you and your friends can think of something to entertain yourselves, say for the rest of the day, weekend or summer." It was just a wonderful time and place to be a kid, and I had my very own front window view right there on 19th Avenue.

19ᵀᴴ Avenue – San Francisco

I lived my entire childhood and adolescence in the same house on 19th Avenue in San Francisco during the late 1940s and 1950s. Our house was one of those long, skinny stucco and wood structures that were lined up one right after another in the fog belt side of San Francisco's Sunset District. To this day, I can recall the sights, sounds, textures and general feeling I had living all of my formative years in that house.

Jim Mullany
First Communion – 1952

I recall a special little perch that I established at our living room window up on the second floor. This was my window to the world and my living room entertainment center. From my lookout window, I could sit on a pillow or a small stool and see all the way to the Pacific Ocean about a mile away, as all the houses between ours and the beach very conveniently sloped down below our house. This viewpoint afforded me an excellent panoramic view all the way to the Farallon Islands, about fifteen miles off the coast.

However, many days the fog billowing in from the ocean afforded me only the visibility of a few blocks, but that was fine with me. I just loved that spot in the front room because it was my very own lookout perch and I could literally watch the world go by.

19th Avenue was a six-lane street that was one of the busiest on the west side of San Francisco, as it was the major west side link to the Golden Gate Bridge. I could watch cars, buses, trucks, and motorcycles pass beneath my window any hour of the day or night. I recall the steady continuous hum from the stream of traffic, interspersed with a symphony of honking horns, the loud blasts and burps from the diesel engines of the buses and trucks, the sirens from emergency vehicles, and screeching of tires when brakes had to be suddenly applied. Some of my friends would question me at times as to how we could stand living on such a busy, noisy street, but it was just something I was so used to, it was just a kind of background music. It provided me with great drama and entertainment. It was a great show that was sometimes punctuated with high drama like car accidents, police chases, occasional motorcades, and I even recall a few times when movies or television shows were filmed there.

I think the unique magic of my perch was its proximity to a special place just beyond the traffic of 19th Avenue. It was a childhood paradise, Larson Park, two square city blocks of playgrounds, playing fields, trees and shrubbery. My childhood was pretty much played out in that park. I recall those days as a glorious time when children had the freedom and safety to actually be children without much oversight from parents and other adults. My first memory of my experiences at Larson Park was of one of my parents

My ballfield at Larson Park

escorting me across the busy street and then leaving me there for hours to play at the playground. Because I was not allowed to cross the street on my own, I was required to scream at the top of my lungs to call one of them to bring me back home. I later figured out that it was totally impossible for them to hear me across six lanes of traffic, and that they would come to get me based upon their own schedules, totally unrelated to my screaming myself hoarse.

    Over the years, I suspect I spent more time in that park than I did in my own home. In Larson Park, I explored the deepest jungles of Africa, dug to China, climbed mountain peaks, and experienced every imaginable adventure of the American West as a cowboy. In later years within the confines of that park, I hit the home run that won the seventh game of the World Series and threw the winning touchdown pass in numerous football championships. And all of these historic exploits and adventures happened just a few steps from my front door, across those six lanes of city traffic.

Larson Park on 19th Avenue
Our house in rear of the photo
St. Cecelia's Church in the background

Kezar Stadium – San Francisco

*In the mid-1950's I attended
my first ball game at Kezar Stadium*

The small pair of binoculars I pulled out of the box brought me back to my first awareness of the existence of binoculars. It goes back more than fifty years to when I attended my first football game in San Francisco at Kezar Stadium. In the mid-1950s, I became aware of "biknocks", as my father used to call them, when I saw men approaching the stadium carrying them in leather cases hanging around their necks.

I was no more than nine years old when my older brother, Mike, took me to my first football game. We rode the Number 28 bus on 19th Avenue from our house, then transferred to the Number 72 bus on Lincoln Way. It is strange that I can recall the bus numbers from so long ago. Our destination, Kezar Stadium, was located at the east end of Golden Gate Park, and my first and lasting impression of the stadium was the smell of Eucalyptus trees and seagulls, for the stadium was located adjacent to a grove of Eucalyptus trees and was just a few miles from the ocean. The promise of discarded morsels of hot dog buns, peanuts or popcorn from the crowd of spectators seemed to attract a squadron of seagulls that patrolled the areas in and around the stadium.

I cannot recall anything about the football game we attended that day other than I know the San Francisco 49ers were one of the teams. But some lessons I learned that day have stuck with me until this day. The first had to do with the fact that we did not have tickets to the game, so my brother had to instruct me about his strategy and techniques for gaining entrance to the game. The first method was what I would come to call "the adopt a family technique." For this approach, you would spot a family advancing to the gate and you would casually join or mingle with the group so you would look like one of their kids. My brother's advice to me that day is true to this day: "Act like you belong, act like you know what you are doing."

The second strategy he informed me about that day was what I came to call "striking the orphan pose." In this one, you would position yourself close to the gate, standing alone, kicking at the ground with head bowed in a pose to make it look like you have lost your best friend, or at least the adult counterpart. It seemed that without fail, some charitable adult would approach and inquire about your welfare. At this point, you would look up with your very best "Mickey Rooney lost soul look" and mention that your father or brother had left you outside without a ticket to the event. Magically, many times over the years a free ticket would materialize.

My second memory from that day was the battle of cushion boys. At the stadium, in those days five cents were paid as a refundable deposit on all seat cushions that were returned to the concession stand under the stadium. So, throughout the stadium, a legion of ambitious boys roamed looking for cushions to collect for that precious five-cent ransom. Boys being boys, various strategies were employed to secure the prized cushions. Cushions were stealthily grabbed from seats right from under the backside of patrons who happened to stand up at the wrong time throughout the game. Gathering the spoils was just one part of this process, as storing and guarding them was also a required element of the operation. This meant that a team approach had to be devised, with a quick, athletic boy to grab the cushions and a strong big boy to guard the piles of plaid cushions as they accumulated. My lasting impression of that day was an emptying stadium with haphazard piles of cushions scattered throughout, vigilantly guarded by budding entrepreneurs, as scores of enterprising seagulls swooped and scavenged the debris left by the crowd.

Rincon Annex Post Office
San Francisco of the 1960s

My first official job, one where you needed a Social Security card, was at the Rincon Annex Post Office in San Francisco in the early 1960s. I was a student and the postal clerk job was a dream job for a student, with flexible hours, good pay, and medical coverage. Students were hired to augment the regular staff during the heavy daily mail processing periods of the early evenings and to work full time during the Christmas mailing crush. We were called part-time temporary indefinite substitute clerks, and I think the title was invented to remind us of the tentative nature of our employment status. We were distinguished from other postal workers by our blue badges, and we came to be called "blue badges." I somehow managed to hold this job for about five years and it paid my way through college, and the job was quite an education in itself.

The job consisted of a variety of tasks, processing the mountain of mail that found its way to the Rincon Annex every weekday from the thousands of businesses and hundreds of thousands of residents of San Francisco. We unloaded and loaded delivery trucks, hand sorted letters, magazines, and parcels, and operated high-speed sorting and cancellation machines. We had to learn the sorting schemes of thousands of San Francisco addresses, California cities, and areas of the United States and abroad. On top of the normal processing of San Francisco mail, Rincon Annex was also the primary processing center for military mail destined for the troops assigned to the Far East during the Vietnam War.

Military veterans, war protesters, struggling artists and musicians, civil rights workers and career college students worked side by side at Rincon Annex in something of a bubbling cauldron, in a work environment that was unlike any other. Every racial and ethnic group seemed to be represented in the workforce that came together along the San Francisco Embarcadero. Every day was a living sociology or psychology lesson. It helped to provide me with a postgraduate degree in life and people. It was a time when many people of college age and young adulthood were said to be "trying to find themselves," and it seemed that many of my co-workers were conducting that search within the piles of mail and parcels at Mission and Spear Streets in San Francisco.

Although there may have been love fests going on in other places in San Francisco like the Haight-Ashbury or Golden Gate Park, there were times of real tension within Rincon Annex during those times. There were rumors of death threats to supervisors by mail handlers who were fueled by nips at flasks that they carried tucked away in their work aprons. Although the term "going postal" had not become part of the lexicon at that time, it was obvious how the seeds of such conflicts came about when untrained supervisors insensitively pushed defiant workers who were not of the mind to be supervised. I even found time to play a little post office there, as it is where I met Bonnie, my future wife and mother to my children.

Each day provided a real-life education on how to get along with and co-exist with people who were much different from me. The lessons that I learned on my first job at Rincon Annex formed the foundation of interpersonal relationships that have endured to this day.

Rincon Annex Post Office Lobby

Rincon Annex Post office

PASSIONS

"If there is no passion in your life,
then have you really lived?
Find your passion, whatever it may be.
Become it, and let it become you
and you will find great things happen FOR you,
TO you and BECAUSE of you."
Author T. Alan

What Do I Need?

  For just about all of my life I have been a part of a family group. I have been a son, brother, husband, father, teammate, airman, and coworker. These rules have provided me with identity, context, texture, and depth as to my place in the world. So now for one of the first times in my life, I am living totally on my own, apart from the family and groups that have helped to provide me with these identities. So, what do I really need now that I am on my own?

  I need the ringing of the telephone, the musical harmony of my cell phone, the beeping alert on my computer alerting me of a new e-mail message, that "snail" mail in my post office box, or the quiet knock upon my door. Yes, I now realize I really need those telephone calls from daughters, siblings, friends, and relatives. The message or content might just be one of the "nothing new, so how about you?" variety. Or the words that magically appear on my computer screen when I click on the mouse, which might be just a complaint about the job or gossip about "that person." This is why I need those words, spoken or written.

  I guess the part of me that needs these verbal and written communiqués is just in my genes. After all, I am Irish, and we have the blarney, the gift of gab, and are heirs to a legacy of Joyce, Yeats, and all those monks scribbling away in their monasteries. It comes down to those words: that is what I need.

  In my present state, there are few things that can match the excitement or the anticipation of opening the mailbox or the electronic connection of opening my e-mail box, seeing the seven new messages that have arrived. Or the flashing light and the beeping tone on the telephone that alerts me those new messages are waiting for me just by punching a few buttons. I hope that amidst the pile of notices that I am the winner of a deal of a lifetime; or the missives that say my life will just not be complete without a new credit card; or a plea that somehow my donation will solve the problems of the world; or that there will be what I really need. There will be the words from you.

I am Sorry, But I Love Baseball

I know I should write about my love of art, literature, poetry, ballet, the opera, great sculptures or paintings, something refined, cultured or meaningful, the beauty of nature, or at least Sophia Loren. **I am sorry, please forgive me, but I love baseball.**

Like with any first love, my love of baseball cannot be easily described or understood by others – love is in the eye of the beholder, and I have loved baseball from that day in the early 1950s when I beheld that vision of perfection, the Seals Stadium baseball field at 16th and Bryant Streets in San Francisco. It was love at first sight when my father took me to my first game and I saw the emerald green grass, the diamond shape of the field enclosed with a fence with such advertising signs as "**Hit this Sign and Win a Suit**" and "**17 Reasons Why to Buy Furniture at Redlick's Furniture Store**." The game of baseball had me at "Play Ball" and has held me ever since. Seals Stadium in San Francisco's Mission District was unique in that it was located downwind from two of the most glorious aroma-producing businesses in the city – the Langendorf Bakery and the Hamms Brewery. The aroma of baked bread, pastries, and beer were a constant backdrop at the park. **I am sorry, but I love baseball.**

The sights, sounds, smells of the game are indelibly etched in my mind and my heart: the smell of a freshly oiled leather baseball glove, the gloriously unique sound of wooden bat striking a horsehide-covered ball – called so accurately as the crack of the bat. And don't let me get started on the smell of cooking hot dogs drifting across the stands from a nearby concession stand. **I am sorry, I know my love should be something far more worthwhile, but I love baseball.**

The words, language, and lexicon of the game are another part of baseball that grabs me and refuses to let me go. All of those baseball terms we use in everyday life – hitting a pop fly; striking out; getting to first base; hitting a home run; being in the ballpark; being thrown a curve in life; stuck out in left field; making it to the major leagues; being off base; playing hardball; needing to pinch hit; getting a rain check. **I am sorry it is not Shakespeare, Dickens or Poe, but I just love baseball.**

Oh, the music of baseball just resonates with me and rattles around in my head. "Take Me Out to the Ball Game" just sends chills when I hear it:

"Take me out to the ball game;
Take me out with the crowd.
Buy me some peanuts and Cracker Jacks,
I don't care if I never get back,
Let me root, root, root for the home team,
If they don't win it's a shame.
For its one, two, three strikes, you're out,
at the old ball game."

I am sorry it is not Mozart or Beethoven, **but I just love baseball.**

Poetry has mystified me a bit ever since my high school English teacher explained iambic pentameter and had us memorize sonnets or couplets, but one poem has stuck in my mind:

"Oh, somewhere in this favored land the sun is shining bright;
The band is playing somewhere, and somewhere hearts are light,

And somewhere men are laughing, and somewhere children shout;
But there is no joy in Mudville - mighty Casey has struck out."

I am sorry it is not Shakespeare or Whitman, **but I love baseball.** Call me shallow or superficial for loving baseball, but unlike other pastimes, hobbies or activities, baseball has its philosopher – one Yogi Berra – who quite clearly explained baseball: **"Ninety percent of baseball is one-half mental."**

Upon second thought and upon reflection, I must proclaim – I am not sorry, I love baseball!

AT&T Park

MY BASEBALL DATE

My dating history in high school was a bit spotty; in fact, I hardly dated at all. I attended an all-boys parochial school in San Francisco in the early 1960s. And because I was not interested in dating boys, it was rather difficult for me as a somewhat shy and introverted type to meet girls. I was busy in high school with sports as I was on the cross country, basketball and track teams, which took up much of my free time. Furthermore, although I belonged to a coed teen club, the regular meetings and dances were a good place to meet and interact with girls but it was way too stressful for me to invite them out. I had no money, no job, and no car, and it seemed to me those were dating essentials.

I attended some school dances where girls from the nearby all-girls schools attended, but my "dates" were mainly group dates with some of my friends and girls we may have known from our elementary school or the neighborhood. Some of my friends thought I should have been more comfortable with girls because I had three older sisters. Of course, with sisters 12, 10 and 8 years older than me, they were more like caretakers and junior mothers, and my primary relationship with them was as a baby brother to baby sitters. The three of them had moved out of our home by the time I had reached the 8th grade.

During my senior year of high school, I obtained a job with the US Postal Service when I reached the age of 18 in the spring of 1963. I was a part-time temporary clerk and would work four hours after school and also would fill in with fulltime work during the Christmas rush and the summer vacation period. It was a great job for a high school and college student as it provided health and vacation benefits, and the pay was twice the minimum wage at the time - $2.15 an hour. Also, we received premium pay for hours worked after 6 pm and extra pay for working on the weekends. It turned out the post office was where I met girls and started and ended my dating life. This is where I met Bonnie, who would become my wife. Dating at the post office happened "organically" as would be the terminology used today. It was natural, because one would work side-by-side with others in something of a mindless job, which would afford one the opportunity to talk with others while you sorted or distributed mail and parcels at a conveyor belt or working as a team at a cancellation machine or stacking station. It was at one of these stacking machines where I got to know Bonnie.

Bonnie was 19 years old and attending City College of San Francisco and I was 21 years old attending San Francisco State College, and we were assigned to work together at a stacking machine on the mezzanine on a Saturday evening. Saturdays were slow days at the PO (as everyone called the post office). We worked side-by-side for 4 hours; by the end, there was pretty much the assumption that we would be going out together. Working together over time brought us together – as my father jokingly referred to it, we got to play post office at the post office. In 1968 we were married, and that was the end of my dating experiences for about 30 years.

After having two daughters and being married for 27 years, Bonnie and I separated in the mid-1990s. It was uncertain, at least to me, that we would ever get back together. I joined a support group of separated, divorced and widowed adults. The joke was in a marital separation there were dumpers and dumpees – for the most part those in the support group were dumpees. Among the general guidelines or advice we were given was not to jump into any rebound relationship as we dealt with the various issues of our previous one. I had a few casual dates during this time, but they were just to have coffee or a meal together. I used some of the time of the early separation to research my family history and do some genealogy. I even took a couple of trips to Ireland. One trip was a two-week tour of Ireland with my sister and brother-in-law in 1996. The very next year I attended a genealogy meeting of Mullanys in our ancestral home in County Roscommon, which was in Ireland known as a "clan rally." Through this group, I met a couple from

Reno. The wife thought we may have been distant relatives with our San Francisco roots. She invited me to come to Reno for a St. Patrick's Day celebration and a clan meeting.

It was fun marching in the St. Patrick's Day parade in Virginia City and visiting the bars afterward. I was introduced to Grazia, a lady from Chile, of primarily Italian descent. She even had a bit of the Irish humor, as she said that her 6% Irish DNA entitled her to march in the parade and drink Guinness and Irish whiskey. It was a great day – I even had an Irish doctor offer to write a note to my employer so I could get the following day off on 'Irish sick leave' as he called it. Grazia gave me her phone number in Reno, and I surprised even myself when I called her for a date a week or so later. We became long-distance friends and companions – she living in the Sierras while I was living on the Monterey Peninsula.

Was this my last date? Or so I thought, until someone surprisingly asked me, "**Hey, maybe sometime we could go to a ball game together**?" I was a bit surprised when I was asked this question by Brian, a guest in Illia Thompson's writing class. He was attending with Carleen, a woman from Woodside who was checking out the class. I am not exactly sure why Brian asked me this question, it may have been because I was wearing my San Francisco Giants cap. We talked briefly and exchanged e-mail addresses. I first thought nothing would come of this suggestion, and then I started thinking – was this going to be my first guy baseball date? Brian seemed like a nice fellow about my age, but what did I know about him and his background? What kind of fan was he? Who was his team? Where had he established his fan credentials? Did he even have fan credentials?

I thought back to my first trip to a ball game at Seals Stadium in San Francisco in the mid-1950s with my dad. The Seals were San Francisco's minor league team before the major league Giants had moved to the City in 1958. The only baseball games I had seen were in black and white on television. So, I was transfixed and amazed when I entered the stadium and saw how beautiful the green grass of the field was in contrast to the brown dirt of the infield. Adding to the day's experience was the fact I learned my dad had grown up about three blocks from the park in the Mission District. We even stopped in for a visit with my Uncle Leo, who had a printing company near the location of my dad's childhood home. Just the baseball at Seals Stadium would have been enough, but right next to the Stadium was the Hamm's Brewery and the Langendorf commercial bakery. So, it was almost magical that above the stadium a large five-story neon beer glass would constantly fill with neon amber beer throughout the game and the sweet aroma of baking bread would permeate the stadium. For years, I thought this was the way it was at all ballparks – neon beer and baking bread aroma.

     Each one of my sisters would have the experience of escorting me to baseball games at Seals Stadium when I was a young boy. They said that I could be anal, stubborn and annoying on the trips to the game. For one thing, when I first started following baseball I had heard the saying, **"The game is not over until the last out is made."** Each one said they had experienced trying to get me to leave early in a game due to the weather or a particularly long game. They said every time that I had stubbornly refused to leave, repeating my mantra – **"The game is not over until the last out has been made."**

     I recall my last baseball date. It was back in the late 1960s and it was what I might call a "courtesy date." In my mind, it was a date when you are regularly dating someone and you agree to go somewhere or do something you would not normally choose to do on your own. For me, it might be to attend the ballet or the opera, something about testosterone. In this case, my girlfriend Bonnie was not a baseball fan, but out of courtesy she went to a baseball game with me. Bonnie was the oldest of her four sisters living at home, so she brought along her twelve-year-old sister Patty. We had a fun day attending an afternoon San Francisco Giants game at Candlestick Park, eating peanuts, popcorn, and hot dogs. Although Candlestick was somewhat notorious for its windy, cold weather, I recall this day was bright. Sunny and warm. The girls seemed to be enjoying themselves as the game ended with a Giants win. As they started to gather up their stuff to go, I surprised them by asking where they were going? Apparently, they did not understand the meaning of a "doubleheader" and did not understand there was a second game. They suddenly dropped the look of good cheer and both said in unison, **"Another game?"** I told them that meant we got to see two games for the price of one. If one game was good, surely two games for the price of one had to be even better. For the baseball fan, this was the greatest of deals.

For the non-fan, this was something quite different. If looks could kill, I would have been a dead man right there in the left field bleachers.

Brian and I exchanged e-mails and we arranged our date. It would be an afternoon game at AT&T Park, the jewel of a baseball field that had replaced Candlestick Park. The joke among Giants fans had been that Candlestick Park "might have been a dump, but it was our dump." The park was so infamous for its cold evening temperatures, the fans who survived night extra-inning games would be given the "Croix de Candlestick," a button modeled on a French medal for heroism, with icicles hanging off the Giants' logo with a photo of fans wrapped in blankets and hoodies. In contrast, Brian and I spent a warm day in the sunshine at AT&T Park watching the Giants play the San Diego Padres in a modern baseball park with many throwback features. Brian, who had retired to the San Francisco Bay Area from Pittsburgh, proclaimed all the right notes in praising the beauty and location of the Park that were music to the ears of this fan of the Giants and San Francisco native.

Brian and I got along well as we shared information about our past lives as fans growing up and of the trials and tribulations of growing old by comparing notes on our orthopedic operations. For Brian, sadly it was a knee replacement that had not gone well and was still causing him pain a year later as he considered a second one. For me, it was a hip replacement after a lifetime of dealing with hip dysplasia. But we preferred talking about our favorite teams. For Brian, it was the Pittsburgh Pirates of days gone by, and for me it was the black and orange Giants. The day we spent together at the ball park turned out to be a fine day, and as we went our separate ways we even talked about our second date – a Giants-Pirates game in August of 2018.

*Croix de Candlestick Medals
Awarded to the Hardiest of Giants Fans
Who Survived a Night Extra Inning Game at Candlestick Park*

A Passion For Books

"I cannot live without books." Thomas Jefferson said it, and I think I have lived it, with a passion for books as long as I can remember. A passion – a powerful emotion, a boundless enthusiasm, fervor, zeal, a strong devotion, a driving attraction. All of these definitions came from – a book. All of these definitions describe how I feel about books, words, and reading. Bookstores, libraries, and other places of books are the candy stores of my life. Books are my addiction, my drugs of choice. Mysteries, histories, memoirs, novels, biographies, travel sagas, sports stories and short stories, anthologies, books about animals, books about books, all are just a few of the types that fill my bookshelves and bookcases to overflowing. I have bought more books than I can ever hope to read in a lifetime, but they provide me a comfort and companionship that makes perfect sense to me.

I ask myself, where does this passion for books come from? How does one explain a passion? I think I was hooked on books and reading ever since I encountered Dick, Jane, and Spot. Although I think my parents both enjoyed reading, they were generally too busy supporting and raising a family of five children to do much pleasure reading from what I can recall. For them, their reading mainly consisted of newspapers and magazines.

I just don't think we are meant to analyze our passions too closely or to really understand them. But a clue to where my passion for reading and books originates may come from my Irish ancestors and their love for storytelling and words. My father was one of eight brothers, and there were some strong ties to writing, books, and words among them. Two of the brothers were newspapermen, one was an English professor, one owned a printing business, and my father dealt in letters for more than forty years

– at the post office. And we all know that letters make words and words make sentences and sentences make paragraphs and what do groups of paragraphs become?

Mania, obsession, passion, a love for books? How else would one describe it? Knowing that I have hundreds of books that I have not read filling my bookshelves at home, I go to bookstores solely to browse, just to look, when it always happens. Books on display or on shelves call out to me – Buy me! Buy me! And of course, I do. But it is comforting to know that I am not unique or alone in this passion when I read this quote:

"When I get a little money, I buy books;
And if any is left, I buy food and clothes."

This came from Erasmus in the sixteenth century. So, I guess my love of books and reading is nothing new or unique.

The love and passion for books may be something I cannot or should not easily explain or describe. It is just one of those things that you know it when you have it or see it. What else can it be when one keeps a journal of almost thirty years, listing books read and with capsule summaries of them along with a personalized rating system. Oh, and did I happen to mention my bookmark collection?

"Books to the ceiling,
Books to the sky.
My pile of books
Is a mile high?
How I love them!
How I need them!
I will have a long beard
By the time I read them." (Arnold Lobel)

Or as Groucho Marx once said,
>*"Outside of a dog, a book is man's best friend,*
>*Inside of a dog, it is just too dark to read."*

MY FAVORITE BOOKS:

Look Homeward Angel – Thomas Wolfe

A Tale of Two Cities – Charles Dickens

Grapes of Wrath – John Steinbeck

In Cold Blood – Truman Capote

Cannery Row – John Steinbeck

Shoeless Joe – W.P. Kinsella

Ian Rankin – John Rebus Mysteries

Michael Connelly – Harry Bosch Series

The House of Sand and Fog – Andre Dubus III

"Mr. Pop"
Jim's personalized Bobblehead

Bobbleheads

As far as fads go, bobbleheads are rather modest compared to some such things as happy face decorations, platform shoes, the mini skirt or Tickle Me Elmo. Bobbleheads are those small caricature dolls representing celebrities or athletes in which the oversized heads are connected to the bodies by a small spring in such a way that a light tap will make the head bobble or wobble, hence the name bobblehead. In the world of fads or unique collectibles a memorable, catchy and creative name helps in my mind to create the uniqueness of an item; for instance, who is going to forget the hula hoop, yo-yos, beanie babies, bell bottoms, go-go boots and leisure suits? In terms of collectibles, bobbleheads are a perfect fad, they are frivolous, silly and have no real intrinsic value or socially redeeming quality except to those who collect them.

Bobbleheads go back to the 1950s, and my first memory of them was of those little doggie dolls people put in their rear car windows whose heads would bobble as the car moved along. In the 1960s some sports teams came up with the idea of oversized bobbleheads as mascots or as a way to publicize a star player. But these bobbleheads were unique and one-time promotional items and did not catch on as a real collectible until 1999. And this is where I come into the picture of the world of bobbleheads quite by accident. Some events in our lives seem predestined to happen or happen by some cosmic karma that we cannot really explain. Such it was with bobbleheads and me.

My nephew and I attended a San Francisco Giants game in 1999 at Candlestick Park which turned out to be a momentous day in bobblehead history, for on this day the San Francisco Giants became the first professional sports team to offer a bobblehead giveaway by distributing 35,000 Willie Mays bobbleheads. The cosmic-karma aspect was that Willie Mays was my favorite baseball player growing up, and in a previous essay, I recounted a ride I received from the great Mays from the ballpark to his home in San Francisco. Also, like many young boys in the 1950s, I had a baseball card collection that may have been worth hundreds of thousands of dollars had it survived. But unlike many boys, it was not my mother who threw away the collection. It was my father who was the culprit when he burned them, including my prized Mays cards, with some trash while I was in the service. Somehow, apparently because of the limited number of Mays bobbleheads produced, they became collectibles and valuable as other sports teams began offering bobblehead promotional giveaways.

  Over the next few years my nephew became fanatical in his mania for collecting bobbleheads, so we always planned our attendance at San Francisco Giants games to coincide with bobblehead giveaways. As a result, over the years my collection grew to more than twenty-five bobbleheads. So, what does one do with one's collection of bobbleheads? My nephew's wife joked that she did not want to know if it came down to her or his bobbleheads. In my case, there was no natural storage or display area in my home for my bobbleheads (translation: my wife and daughters vetoed the idea of a bobblehead display in the house) and they remained stored in a cardboard box until fate intervened in the form of an office move on my job in Sacramento. While most in my branch in my State of California office complained about our move to modular cubicles, the top of my bookshelves offered a perfect home for my collection of bobbleheads. As many who have worked in a cubicle office environment have discovered, the efficient use of space developed by some office efficiency designer can be very impersonal and dehumanizing. So many workers forced into these cubicles sought ways to personalize them. In my case, populating my cubicle with bobbleheads seemed a perfect response to an office arrangement obviously developed by a bobblehead.

  Just as the bobblehead collection fad had been both unanticipated and unplanned, so too was what happened when my bobblehead collection was introduced to the staid, gray world of state office cubicles. First, the bobbleheads, which sat higher than all the cubicle walls, became an office landmark, as in 'go down to the bobbleheads and turn left', or, 'if you pass the bobbleheads, you have gone too far'. Then they became part of my identity as the bobblehead guy or Mr. Bobblehead. I knew it had gone too far when I received a phone call from a federal government representative in Washington DC and he wanted to know if I was the bobblehead guy. Amazingly, the bobbleheads made their way into my work when two co-workers used some of the bobbleheads in an educational video that publicized the statewide Paternity program I had founded and headed at that time, and ultimately when I retired I achieved bobblehead immortality of my own when I was presented with my own bobblehead.

    When I told my two daughters that I would be presented with a difficult dilemma in my will when I would have to determine which one would be getting my bobbleheads, my youngest daughter told me that my bobblehead was sort of "creepy," almost like one of those scary dolls that come to life in a horror movie.

PEOPLE

*"Sometimes people come into your life for a moment,
a day, or a lifetime. It matters not the time they spend with you,
but how they impacted you in that time."*
Unknown

A Girl Named Erin

Erin Mullany, age 5

What's in a name? What does "name" mean to you? Some research has found that the names we are given carry substantial psychological weight and that our name will define us throughout our lives and may even lay the foundation for our personality. The name Erin is of Gaelic origin and its meaning is Ireland, it is a poetic name for the Island in song and poems. The name means peace and tranquility. When my wife Bonnie and I agreed to name our first child, a daughter, Erin, we were thinking it was a nice Irish name that would go nicely with the last name Mullany. Little did we know that there would be scant little peace and tranquility in our lives for the first few years of baby Erin's life.

I was in the last six months of my Air Force enlistment in January 1973 when Erin Jennifer Mullany was born at March Air Force Base Hospital in Riverside, California. Like all first-time parents, we believed that our Erin would be unique and special. Her entrance into the world *was* pretty special. I battled rush hour traffic to get Bonnie to the hospital just in time to have Erin be delivered within an hour of arrival, feet first – a breech birth. Erin was born during the time when babies were kept in nurseries, a bit away from the mother's room. Bonnie told me that even at a distance she could recognize Erin's unique cry from the other infants in the nursery. I attributed this to some motherly pride or instinct until I came to recognize Erin's scream too, not just because Erin's cry was unique or different, but because it was the loudest and most persistent of them all. You see, although baby Erin weighed less than six pounds at birth, she put every ounce of her being from the tip of her toes to the top of her head into screaming. Peace and tranquility?

Once we brought Erin home to our small one-bedroom apartment in Redlands, California, we discovered that she was the answer to an age-old philosophical question: If a tree fell in the forest and no one was around, who would hear it? Erin would hear it, along with the sounds of a leaf falling from a distant tree or a squirrel running across the grass – Erin would hear all these sounds and she was none too happy to be disturbed. She would scream day and night in response to these disturbing sounds. And periods of sleep were rare for her mother and me for the first six or seven months of her life. We grew to fear her little head starting to bob up and down and her ears starting to turn red, for those were the warning signs that a noise had disturbed her and she was about to unleash the full power of her lungs to fill our apartment with high decibel screams. But this was just the beginning of our life with Erin. Peace and tranquility?

The word that best described Erin in her early years was feisty – but the words spirited, spunky, pugnacious, frisky, fiery, excitable, sassy, full of energy, adventuresome and extremely curious all seemed to fit our young Erin. Some of the escapades and adventures we experienced with Erin during her first four years were:

- A couple of trips to the emergency hospital when Erin was able to sample ant poison and snail bait despite all of our precautions and safety measures;
- The time as a three-year-old when Erin was discovered to be vigorously chewing gum that we knew was not available in our home; when questioned about the origin of the gum, Erin admitted she had pried the gum off the sidewalk using a a butter knife. When cautioned about how dirty the gum could be and that dogs could have peed on it, Erin proclaimed knowingly that she had closely observed the gum for a period of time and "**that no dogs had peed on it**";
- Erin was a devotee of Mr. Rogers's neighborly friendliness with an attitude; when some neighbors did not respond to her soft-spoken "Hi, Neighbor", this tiny child would become belligerent and would sometimes scream at the startled adults, **"I said, Hi Neighbor!"**;
- Erin knew that her mother and I were opposed to smoking, so at the age of three or four she responded to a disagreement with us by loudly proclaiming "**and also, I am going to smoke**;"
- Once she announced, "**I am going to paint!**" When told she could not use our house paint in the garage, she very quietly proceeded to paint the hood of her mother's car with Super Glue;
- One idea we had was when Erin misbehaved, we took away one of her favorite toys and place it in the rafters in the garage so that she would be able to see it and be motivated to do better in the future to get the toy back. We realized our idea

had backfired when we overheard Erin telling her little friend "and that little bike is up there from when I said a bad word", "and that little dolly is there for when I did not pick up my toys". It was almost like she was proudly giving tours of her misbehavior to her little friends. A friend of ours who had studied child psychology said she believed Erin had personally disproved a number of child psychology theories;

- Once due to miscommunication with the mother of one of her playmates, Erin and her little playmate went missing when she was about four years old. The police had to be notified, and for about two hours a frantic search was being conducted when Erin and her friend Christina emerged from a neighbor's house. Apparently, they had been playing at a little friend's house while the friend was at kindergarten, and the mother there did not know the two had been reported as missing. When the episode had concluded, the policeman gave the two little girls a mild lecture about the importance of telling their parents where they were. Erin's little friend shook and started to cry. When the policeman asked Erin if she would always let her mother know where she was, tiny Erin stared at the towering policeman and calmly said, "**I don't have to.**"

Fortunately, Erin got most of this out of her system by age six, and she has grown up to be a very compassionate, generous, kind and loving daughter, although she has retained a bit of her feistiness. Recently when I suffered a mild stroke, Erin sent me the most beautiful note a father could ever receive from an adult child. It was ironic in that I had been forming the contents of this essay in my head when I went to sleep on the night I suffered the stroke. Erin concluded her note by writing:

"I want to tell you I am sorry for being difficult and feisty at times. I think I have made a huge improvement from when I was younger, but I am still a work in progress. I love you very much and hope you have a Happy Birthday. Here's to twenty more years of memories!!!!!"

And Erin, I am so grateful and fortunate to have you as my daughter.

Erin, age 4 in San Francisco

THE QUIET ONES

I was the youngest child of five, born into a large, Irish Catholic family in San Francisco, California in the mid-1940s. During those times, I was not sure there was any other type of Irish Catholic family back in those days. I had three older sisters – Ann, who was eleven years older, Maureen, ten years older, Lucille, eight years older, and my brother Mike who was four years older than me. My parents and siblings were world-class talkers. And not only could they talk, but they were all loud talkers and talking was like a competitive sport in my family. On the other hand, I was shy and quiet and often when

the family referred to me, I was referred to as the quiet one or the shy one. Like many shy or quiet kids, I detested it whenever someone in the family referred to me or point me out as the quiet one. It was as if I had a disease or a personal deficiency. Later in my life, the term 'introverted' came into use to refer to people who were shy or quiet, although with the term 'introvert' there was a subtle difference that being quiet was a matter of choice. For me, it was just the way I was, as I had anxiety or fear whenever I was called upon to speak. I neither knew what to say nor did I have anything to say. I had always thought it was a genetic thing, something I was born with, although in my family the environment was definitely a contributing factor.

    I was comfortable talking inside my home, with my family. The only problem was I lived with six world-class talkers and there were very few opportunities to talk. My sisters had established their own conversation long before I was born and I was never asked to join their conversations, nor did I have any inclination to do so. In fact, to this day when I am with my sisters, their conversation is still something of a mystery to me. Names, events and the situations they talk about are usually not familiar to me. With my brother Mike, he thought that he was our family's answer to Jerry Lewis and his jokes and funny stories filled up the room, and I was symbolically pushed into a corner. My mother's talking was usually to family and friends via the telephone. She could talk for hours on the phone and it was not easy to get her attention during one of her four- or six-hour marathon sessions on the phone. Although my father shared funny stories or would tell us one of his theories on life, his real talking was reserved for the unsuspecting store clerks, gas station attendants or strangers waiting for the bus; or he was particularly adept at turning the tables on Jehovah Witness or Mormon proselytizers who came to our front door. I think they were a bit surprised when he invited them in to discuss Catholic theology.

    When I went to school things were even worse, as I lived in fear of being called upon to recite or called to the blackboard to solve a math problem. To me, it was terrifying when faced with how to just to figure out how to write left-handed on the chalkboard without out the added stress of talking in front of the class at the same time. As a lefty, we had never been taught how to write at the blackboard. I quickly learned that neither in my family nor in society in general was being the "quiet one" viewed as positive or a normal condition. Thinking back on those childhood days, being quiet or shy was not a condition that neither my family nor the school system were equipped to deal with. I felt different or odd being the quiet one; sometimes I was lonely. On the other hand, I preferred to be alone at times and not to be noticed, even within my family. I loved to read, play with my army men and keep score of baseball and basketball games. Most of the time I was just more comfortable and relaxed when I was alone.

Also, in my large noisy family I was happy not to be noticed, to be almost invisible, because I did not want to be noticed or visible. I felt comfortable with this role as the incessant talk swirled around me. And, being the quiet one and the invisible one as the baby in the family afforded me the opportunity to be the silent observer, the eavesdropper, the spy who was able to pick up family secrets and idiosyncrasies. Although there were seven of us, we had only three bedrooms and one split bathroom and a large living room and dining room (both of which were mainly for display purposes or for when we had company). The split bathroom had a small toilet room and a larger room that contained a bathtub, shower, washing sink, and medicine cabinet. The two areas of the bathroom were separated by a small niche that contained our telephone and a small fold-out shelf that could be used as a writing surface. This niche was primarily the domain of my mother, as she was the one who most often used the telephone. Sitting quietly on the toilet seat afforded me numerous opportunities to hear about family news, gossip, and secrets, although being quiet and shy, I very seldom revealed the family secrets or gossip I heard. Just knowing them was enough for me. I think the early seeds for me becoming a special investigator with the state were likely planted on that toilet seat. An added bonus of that location was with our row house slapped right against the house of our neighbors, the Harrington's. I was able to pick up some real Harrington family tidbits also. However, this feature was known to all of the family and the source of much information and family entertainment whenever anyone in the family used the toilet. Hearing all of the Harrington's arguments, family problems and secrets may have been my first clue to the fact that all Irish-Catholic families were dysfunctional – not just my own.

My first breakthrough from being the quiet or shy one was through sports. At Saint Cecilia's School and in my neighborhood (I lived right around the corner from the school), all my friends were boys who were both classmates and neighbors, and our friendship was built upon sandlot sports and games. I felt comfortable with these friends and with the games we played. I was neither shy nor had any anxieties around sports. When I advanced to organized Catholic Youth Organization sports, I had the good fortune of being with an incredible group of athletes on St. Cecilia's baseball and basketball teams. From my participation in these sports, I gained some personal confidence, and for me it was like playing a role. I was not the quiet one when I was on these teams. This role continued through high school, where I found my group of friends on track and cross-country teams at Riordan High School, an All-Boys Parochial School.

But I still considered myself shy and quiet in certain situations. In class when called upon to recite, or around adults or people I did know well, and around girls – well, forget about it, I was almost paralyzed. But as I grew and matured, a subtle change came about. I went from an anxious, shy person to an introvert, or one who preferred to be alone when faced with boring social events or with people I did not care to be around. I no longer fully felt that I was the one with the problem for not speaking and that it might really have been the problem of the ones who talked incessantly when they actually had nothing to say.

One day, my mother mentioned that my dad was extremely shy when he was a young man when they were dating. I was shocked to learn that this man who I knew as a world-class talker who could talk to anyone, in any situation on almost any topic, was once the quiet one! But then I thought about what he must have been like as a young man born into a family of eight boys and two immigrant parents from Ireland – and everyone knew how the Irish could talk. I continue to believe that being shy or introverted was a condition you were born with, but also one that was influenced by your family and your environment.

Some of the mysteries and questions about being the shy one or the quiet one came into focus when my younger daughter Adrienne arrived. As a baby and toddler, Adrienne was calm, sweet, contented and quiet. She was a happy baby with a laugh that we all called her chortle, as that is how she laughed. As she approached kindergarten age, my wife and

I noticed that Adrienne was quiet and shy outside of the family, although we were happy she had a couple of little friends whom she played with regularly. We never pointed out or identified her as the shy one or the quiet one or pointed out that she was different from any of the other kids. But things did change when she started kindergarten and had to face more of the outside world. On one of the first parent-teacher conferences, my wife Bonnie attended to consult with Adrienne's kindergarten teacher. The issue of some teachers not being able to understand or work with the shy child came right to the surface. The kindergarten teacher told Bonnie that she should have Adrienne see a counselor, and the inference was that Adrienne was "slow." Bonnie, who had volunteered at the school and was familiar with the methods of most of the teachers, was incensed. She confronted the teacher about what evidence she had that Adrienne needed to see a counselor, and the teacher said Adrienne was so quiet and also that she was not able to identify the parts of the body. Bonnie brought Adrienne right over and Adrienne quickly identified the clavicle, sternum, phalanges and almost every other body part. Bonnie confronted the teacher about the teacher's training and what qualifications she had to identify a "slow child." This slow child later obtained a Bachelor of Science Degree in Biology from UC Davis and worked in the legal field, specializing in the area of trademarks, copyrights, and intellectual property. This would be the first and last time Adrienne was identified as needing counseling during her academic career.

 One of our main concerns with having a shy child was if she was happy and if she was able to fit in at school socially, as she never had any problems with academics. We became convinced that being shy or quiet was just her nature and personality, something she had been born with. I was happy and pleased as Adrienne advanced to middle school and then to a high school, where the extra-curricular activities she participated in were track and cross country. I had told her that these were fun sports where everyone got to participate and where you could make some good friends, as that had been my experience in school. I was very happy when she participated in these sports for four years in high school, and to this day she is still a runner. She made good friends and the coed teams became like her family.

After college graduation, Adrienne moved from Sacramento to Silicon Valley where she found a job in the legal department of the tech firm Rambus and was later introduced to a young man named Joel. Much like her dad, she went on to become engaged in her first serious relationship. Joel described himself as "a nerd" and seemed like the perfect mate for Adrienne. As Adrienne was the first of our two daughters to be married, I was very excited to be the Father of the Bride. I thought I had the perfect role model in Steve Martin from the movie "Father of the Bride". But I had a bit to learn about being Father of the Bride. In the movie, the Steve Martin character and his daughter had a very touching scene where they talked about this milestone event in their lives the night before the wedding while playing basketball in the backyard. So, using this as my example, I proposed that Adrienne and I could go out for a run on the Monterey Peninsula the morning of her wedding. She responded: "Dad, are you out of your ever-loving mind? Do you have any idea the preparations a bride has before her wedding?" She then told me she was going to have to start her preparations at dawn for her 11:00 am wedding. She proceeded to tell all that she needed to do, and I got the point at her mention of the pedicure or manicure.

    She had gone over my duties and responsibilities for the wedding weekend as the Father of the Bride. Because Joel's family was coming from Ohio and many of his college friends were coming from outside of California, I was designated the informal host for these visitors. Also, I learned that it was a tradition for the Father of the Bride to give the wedding toast and a little speech about the new couple. Adrienne had strongly cautioned me, telling me that Joel and she were private people and any speech or toast by me should respect that.

    Unfortunately, Adrienne failed to factor the lethal combination – a man of Irish descent, a microphone and the sentimentality brought on by the lethal combination of champagne and beer. The family had a nice video made about the early lives of Adrienne and Joel which I introduced at their rehearsal dinner. I thought that I had exercised restraint during the speeches and the toast. In fact, Joel's dad mentioned that I had set the bar for wedding speeches. I just am not sure if he said I set that bar high or low.

A few years after their wedding, I was invited to join Joel's family football pool. It was a tradition in his family to have a contest to predict the outcome of football games throughout the year, with a small monetary prize to the winner. Joel's uncle Tom was the commissioner, and as such, he set up and ran the weekly pool. Because I was in California and most of the participants were in the Midwest, the pool was conducted over the Internet. Tom had the power to assign nicknames to all in the pool, and those names would be how we would be known to all participants. I was shocked when the nickname he assigned to me was "Jabberin' Jim!" I called my daughter Adrienne right away to ask how Joel's uncle came to call me "Jabberin' Jim". Her only response was, "Dad, he heard your speeches at the wedding."

I had gone from the "quiet one" to "Jabberin' Jim" in my lifetime, and somewhere, my dad was smiling.

Adrienne Jones (Mullany) with Dad
Wedding Day, August 21, 2004

PINKY – MY BEST FRIEND

My very first friend in life turned out to be my best friend for life. He started out as Bobby, was transformed to Pinky, and eventually became Bob during our years together. My earliest memory of Bobby was one of my first memories of my life. We must have been about three or four years old when our mothers brought us together as playmates in the late 1940s. We lived about a half a block apart on 19th Avenue in San Francisco and we were both about the same age, so I guess it was natural for our mothers to bring us together. But they could never have imagined the friendship we would form over the next twenty years.

Bobby was chubby, blond and very friendly and outgoing, while I was a shy, skinny boy with light brown hair. We were total opposites in almost every way imaginable. He was made to be noticed, while I wanted to be invisible.

One of our first adventures together put our friendship to the test. We were assigned to different kindergarten classes when we started school at St. Cecilia's School. Bobby made it known from the outset that he was not happy with this arrangement and that he wanted to be in my class. But little did I know the extent he would go to in order to get his way and be in my class until I heard loud, piercing screaming coming from his classroom. I was horrified when I learned that it was Bobby who was making the ruckus and that I was the focus of his outburst. He screamed, kicked and cried out that he wanted to be in "Jimmy's class." I wanted to disappear when the connection was finally made that I was "the Jimmy" he was crying about. As I was to learn throughout our friendship, Bobby usually got his way, as he would make lots of noise and create a ruckus until things worked out as he wished. Bobby just had a magical way of charming adults.

In later years at parochial school, we somehow became altar boy partners for four years due to our being the exact same height in the fifth grade. I always wanted our altar boy service to go quietly and unnoticed, so I regularly had to school him in the proper Latin responses and our designated assignment at Mass or the other services like weddings and funerals. Of course, the more I worried about our performance, the more noticeable and serious his gaffes became, from passing out due to an unexpected heat wave, to falling asleep and snoring loudly at an early morning Mass, to tripping and falling over his church gown and rolling down the alter steps, to major pratfalls. Bobby managed to become what my father called "the greatest show in Church." But these mortifying performances were easily balanced out by his easygoing, friendly nature, his loyal friendship, his generosity and his puppy dog-like effort to please one and all. By the end of our grammar school years, he had become Pinky to one and all, as we found out Pinky was his father's nickname during his minor-league baseball career, and so it was a perfect match for Bobby's fair skin that turned pink during any form of exercise or physical exertion.

Our friendship grew and deepened as we matured through our high school years and attended the same all-boys parochial high school in San Francisco. But as often happens, we just drifted apart after our high school years and we went our separate ways with our own families, careers, and moves to different cities. For the next thirty years or so, we would only come together at school reunions or major events like weddings or funerals. But no matter how long our separations had been, the years would just melt away, and conversation and communication would continue as if there had been no interruptions. As an adult, even though he would become a multi-millionaire stockbroker, Bobby just became an adult version of the kid he had always been. He was a big teddy bear of a man who reminded many of the football sportscaster and former coach, John Madden, in both physical appearance and his friendly disposition – the type of guy you would want to share a beer with while watching the game.

It all came to an end suddenly in a simple offhanded remark buried at the bottom of an e-mail message from my sister, Lou. "Oh, did you hear that your friend Bobby died last week of a heart attack?" I felt like I had been punched in the stomach, and all the air seemed to leak out of my body. I stared at the computer screen and I wept.

Robert "Pinky" Collins

The Mystery of Joe

    I had known Joe as long as I could remember, but did I ever really know Joe? We started out as classmates in the kindergarten class at St. Cecilia's Elementary School in San Francisco and remained classmates throughout elementary and high school. We were classmates and teammates for more than twelve years, but I am not sure whether or not you could define our relationship as friends. Joe played second base on our CYO and recreation league teams – this was before Little League was established. I was always a first baseman. Most of our connections were from being on the same team and for our proximity of being in many of the same classes throughout school. I recall one summer we were even invited to play on an invitational recreation park team being put together by Coach Malloy. Coach Malloy was a well-known recreation director in San Francisco, so it was something of an honor that Joe and I shared, being invited to play on that summer league ball team.

    Joe was always one of the shortest boys in our class, and consequently was always at the front of the line when we lined up according to height. I think because he had been teased and bullied a bit because of his height, he had something of an attitude about his size. I recall some kids saying Joe had the "little man's syndrome." Because we wore school uniforms, I don't think boys during those times paid much attention to clothes and styles. Thinking back on it, Joe's regular clothes seemed to have a hand-me-down quality to them – always a little too big for him and a little more worn out than the clothes of the other boys. I knew that he came from a large family, but he was something of a mystery to me.

    We moved on to Riordan High, an all-boys' parochial high school, and we continued to be classmates and teammates. We had many classes together, and we were both distance runners with the track and cross-country teams. I usually came out ahead of

Joe in races, but he was always a very competitive runner. In the classroom, Joe was challenged; he had trouble with some subjects. At times, it was a struggle for him to maintain his athletic eligibility, and I would sometimes help him with assignments or homework. I always felt he tried and that his struggles were rarely due to a lack of effort. In high school, as Joe matured there were times he was distant, preoccupied and remote. I was never able to penetrate what was beyond the façade with Joe. After high school we went our separate ways; Joe joined the Air Force and I went on to college.

 A year or so after I had graduated from college and Joe had been discharged from the service, we literally ran into each other when we were both out running near Golden Gate Park. I guess running was still a bond between us. I was amazed to see how much Joe had grown and matured during those four years in the service. He was no longer little Joe. He had grown to be a very talented runner, one of the best in the San Francisco Bay Area. Joe recounted in general terms that he had experienced some difficulties in the Air Force while he had been assigned as a base photographer in Libya. He had found a job at the U.S. Postal Service facility in Oakland. I felt that maybe Joe's life was now on course. That feeling lasted until a few months later when I learned that Joe had been fired from the Post Office. Having worked for the post office myself during my college years I knew that it was almost impossible to be fired from the post office. I wondered what happened with Joe.

 More than twenty-five years later I found out what had happened to Joe. I still vividly recall how shocked I was to receive that Sunday morning call in the late 1990s. Joe had tracked me down to Sacramento and was calling to catch up on our lives and the lives of old classmates and teammates. Joe told me in a matter of fact way that he had his ups and downs in life and was currently trying to regain his sobriety. This caught me off guard, for I had never known Joe to have been a drinker. His residential address in San Francisco's Tenderloin was documentary evidence of how far he had fallen. If there was a place in San Francisco that could be identified as lower than rock bottom, where he was living in the center of the Tenderloin was that place. It saddened me to hear how far Joe had fallen, a person whom I had known longer than just about anyone else in my life.

Over the next few years, I received sporadic calls from Joe. He never asked me for anything, he just wanted to talk and update me on the lives of classmates and their families. He seemed to be in contact with many more of them than I was.

The Joe story took a little bit of an unexpected twist about five years ago as our elementary school reunion was being planned. I came to learn that some classmates still in the San Francisco area had been bothered by Joe for money in a way that bordered on harassment. These classmates had raised the issue that if Joe was invited to the reunion they would not attend, and there was some fear that he might disrupt the party. We chose to invite him anyway because we thought that was the right thing to do. It turned out that he made only a token appearance at the function. He seemed withdrawn and distant, almost like he had been sedated in order to be able to attend.

Coincidentally, our high school reunion was held later in the same year. It was a different Joe who attended this event. He was friendly and talkative as we relived the old times and caught up on the last forty years with our classmates. I think he was encouraged by the fact that all eight members of our cross-country team were in attendance, as we had been a tight-knit group in high school. As we walked around on a tour of the campus, Joe stunned me when he very casually revealed to me that he had been molested by Coach Malloy back when we were ten or eleven years old. He disclosed to me the humiliation, embarrassment, and shame he had felt at having to tell his parents, authorities and the court about the events. I recalled having heard the news about the arrest and incarceration of Coach Malloy many years later, but I had never connected those events with Joe or anyone else I know. The mystery of Joe was a mystery no more.

Joe, My troubled classmate and friend

TURNING POINTS – JACOB ANDERSON

    Later, when you look back over your life there will be a few turning points that helped to shape the person you became and what you did with your life. There will be those times when you took that sharp turn to the right. However, there will also be those times when you took that wrong turn in moments that you can never recover or make right.

    Back when I was in my senior year of high school, I started working part-time for the United States Postal Service in San Francisco. My father had told me that if I wanted to attend college I would have to pay for it myself, and the post office job was a perfect one for a student. It not only offered the income to pay for my college education, it offered a different kind of education, one not found in books and classrooms.

    It was during the turbulent 1960s, a time of great unrest and the summers of love in San Francisco. The Rincon Annex Post Office seemed to reflect it all with the diversity and the variety of people who worked there as part-timers, or blue badges as we were called due to the color of our identification badges. From the hippies of the Haight-Ashbury to a racial and ethnic mix that reflected the diversity of the Bay Area, working at the Rincon was a course in real life 101. I met my future wife Bonnie, there, and we became friends with a man who was unlike the rest of the blue badges we worked with.

    His name was Jake or Andy, depending on who he was talking with or who was referring to him, because his given name was Jacob Anderson. Unlike the other part-timers who were in their twenties, Jake was much older, in his late 60s or his 70s. He was something of a father or grandfather figure to us younger people.

Jake was a Dane who had come to America from Denmark back in the 1920s or 1930s. He had worked on farms as a young man, and he had retained a hint of his Danish language accent over the years. I think he was the first man of my parents' generation or age that I had actually become friends with. To most of his co-workers, he was just a kindly figure to encounter at work, and that was about the only interaction they had with him. But for Bonnie and me it was different. He became a friend.

Jake was a humble man with character, dignity and a genuineness that is rarely found in people. I think by some standards he would be considered to be a poor man. His work at the post office was likely out of necessity, as I suspected his only source of retirement income was Social Security. He did not own a car, and from my discussions with him, I wondered if he even knew how to drive. I never heard him complain about his lack of material wealth, nor did I ever hear him speak ill of anyone who had the things he did not. He was one of few men I had ever met who I would call a gentleman and gentle man.

Jake lived on Haight Street amid all of the craziness of the Haight-Ashbury during its heyday, but it did not seem to have touched him. His apartment was on the second floor of an old Victorian house, and he jokingly told us to ring two times when we visited him, as the saying in Denmark was to "ring twice in case of war." Just coming to the place was like a history lesson, as his downstairs neighbor was an elderly Russian who had served in the Russian army back during the revolution.

Jake always put out the few special plates he had and served us Danish pastries and Tuborg Danish beer. He was proud of his heritage and he always shared whatever he had. Jake did not have any immediate family, so I think in a small way we became his family.

We loved listening to his stories about Denmark, coming to America, and the humor he injected into these tales with a twinkle in his eye. He joked about being part of a failed experiment during World War II to see if older men in their forties and fifties could be trained as soldiers. He said he went through a short-lived basic training at Fort Ord and spoke with pride at having hiked from Monterey to the San Francisco Presidio. I know he was very appreciative and happy when we drove him down to the Monterey Peninsula for a visit, telling us how much faster it was than his previous trip.

    In the four years that I was in the Air Force, we drifted apart from Jake. Sometimes we visited him when I was home on leave, or we would sporadically exchange cards or letters. After I was discharged from the military and we had returned to the Bay Area, we decided to pay Jake a visit. We learned that he had moved and was living in a rougher part of town over in the Mission District. We had been unable to reach him by telephone, so we decided to find his apartment and pay him a visit. As Bonnie waited in the car, I went up to the old apartment building to look for Jake. A neighbor came out and I asked him if he knew where Jacob Anderson's apartment was. He said, "Oh, the old man? He had been sick and died about eight months ago." I returned to the car and told Bonnie our friend was dead. We sat in the car for a long time in silence. A part of the silence was our grief, but another part was our shame and regret. We realized that we had been too busy with our lives to have been there for Jake when he had needed us the most. We had allowed him to die alone.

Uncle Gerald
A Family Eccentric

Uncle Gerald

In the late 1890s, an unknown Montgomery street character addressed the San Francisco Board of Supervisors: "G*entlemen, as I look over you, I see that anyone can become a millionaire, but how many of you have the talent to become a character?"*

My father's family of eight boys was a group of one-of-a-kind, throw-away-the-mold, march-to-the-beat-of-their-own-drummer types. They were an assemblage of San Francisco Irish characters who grew up and matured during the Roaring Twenties and the Great Depression. It was a group that asserted their individuality and eccentricities with a form of courage and defiance. They were not afraid of being different – they embraced their individuality almost as a badge of honor.

In a family populated by eccentric characters, my Uncle Gerald was the most eccentric and peculiar member of the Mullany clan. He was a talented and creative writer, an innovative storyteller who devoted his life to journalism. Gerald spent all of his working life as a newspaperman, working for newspapers in Eureka, San Francisco and for most of his career in Los Angeles, where he wrote for the Los Angeles Examiner and Herald-Examiner. I retain a vivid image of him to this day – he was always dressed in a three-piece suit and tie, no matter what the occasion. I don't think anyone in the family had ever seen him without his three-piece suit, and outdoors he always wore a well-aged fedora. His attire always seemed to give him an air of civility and formality, even though his suits and hats seemed to be years out of date and at odds with the style of the day or the occasion.

My fascination with Uncle Gerald and his offbeat personality originated in part from a feeling I had as a child that I somehow shared some of his "uniqueness." I was fascinated by Uncle Gerald because I saw him as an enthralling character who was much different from the adult men I knew in our family when I was growing up. First, there was the fact he was a lifelong bachelor who lived in Los Angeles. Los Angeles? Every other Mullany I knew lived in San Francisco or very close to San Francisco, yet Uncle Gerald lived in Los Angeles, which most San Franciscans viewed as a strange and foreign place. The Mullany men were all married and fathers; Uncle Gerald was a lifelong bachelor who seemed uncomfortable around children. Not only did Uncle Gerald live in Los Angeles, he lived in Downtown Los Angeles in a "residential hotel" with other single adults across the street from Pershing Square and the World-Famous Biltmore Hotel. The men I knew sometimes dressed casually when they worked around the house or went to the beach or fishing. Uncle Gerald always wore that three-piece suit and fedora. I sometimes imagined that he slept in his suit.

The Uncle Gerald stories were legendary in our family. I think some of them may have been exaggerated, but I had heard them so many times they became accepted as part of our family history. Uncle Gerald was known to always carry a rolled-up newspaper whenever he went walking, which was pretty much all the time because he did not own or know how to drive a car. Uncle Gerald always walked swinging that rolled-up newspaper from side to side in order to fend off any other pedestrians who strayed too close to his "sidewalk space" as he called it.

He ate all of his meals in self-serve cafeterias, his favorite being Clifton's on Olive Street in downtown Los Angeles. Every evening he ate dinner at this cafeteria and he claimed the same seat. My father said Uncle Gerald once stood over a fellow diner while holding his tray, and when the fellow inquired as to what Gerald wanted, Gerald responded that the other man was in his seat and he suggested the other diner might consider moving to another location.

Gerald's background in the newspaper business in the entertainment capital of the west provided him with a wealth of stories to tell. He loved to talk and tell stories. He was a great storyteller but a not too great listener. And it was not just the stories he told that made Uncle Gerald unique, but also his method of delivery. First,

Uncle Gerald was a loud talker and he never realized he was a loud talker. Next, he was something of a stutterer – Uncle Gerald was a situational stutterer. The more excited he was about a story he was telling or the closer he came to the punch line, the louder he got and the more pronounced his stutter became. And the third element of his presentations made his stories come across like a performance of a one-man band. Uncle Gerald had a complete set of ill-fitting false teeth. The faster and louder he talked, the more pronounced the click-clacking of his false teeth became. My father liked to refer to Gerald's false teeth clicking as his personal set of castanets.

A ritual and a routine had evolved and developed over the years for Uncle Gerald's once- or twice-a-year visits to the homes of his brothers, who all lived in Northern California and who all had families, while Gerald was a bachelor living in Southern California. Gerald's visits virtually amounted to solo performances where he was prepared to unload the months of stories he had stored up for these visits. I recall thinking he was like a human relay baton that was passed along from brother to brother as he exhausted his time in each household.

I recall the visits to our home in San Francisco followed a ritual that must have been established years prior to my birth. Uncle Gerald was one of the oldest of the brothers, having been born in 1899, and the visits I recall took place in the 1950s and early 1960s. In our house, my mother must have established the rules for Gerald's visits, as he was there to drink beer or hard liquor with my father and his stories were clearly intended for his brothers. After a perfunctory and polite greeting between my mother and Uncle Gerald, he and my father would quickly withdraw to the downstairs basement or spare room far away from the central living space in our two-story home. Gerald's stories were liberally sprinkled with some mild expletives, and they flowed more frequently depending upon the duration and strength of the drinking.

But Uncle Gerald was a loud talker, and the walls and floors between him and the rest of the family gathered upstairs could rarely mute the level of his voice below a mild roar. So, his visits took on a pattern: Gerald's stories would escalate in volume and my mother would either scream down the stairs at the two brothers to lower the volume, or she would say that the kids were trying to sleep or study. But that tactic seldom silenced Gerald or my father, so the next step was to raise the volume of the television or radio in order to drown out Gerald or my father's volume, which of course only made them talk louder to be heard over the television or radio. This would go on for a time until finally the phone call would be made. I am not sure how my father would get the word out, but at some point, he would come upstairs and quietly call one of his brothers to tell them it was time for them to come over and pick up Uncle Gerald. The baton was being passed. Because Gerald was a journalist living in Los Angeles, it seemed that he never ran out of stories to tell.

One story my father loved to tell us about Gerald came in the context of the fact that most of the Mullany brothers had been too young to serve in World War I and too old to serve in World War II. Except for Uncle Gerald, who was the sole Mullany brother to serve in the US Military. In 1918, Uncle Gerald was enrolled at the University of California, Berkley, in the Journalism program and was also a member of the Army ROTC program. My father told the story that it was his participation in the ROTC program that led to Uncle Gerald's "distinguished" military career during World War I. On November 5, 1918, Gerald began his active duty service with the United States Army, and on November 11, 1918, at the eleventh hour of the eleventh day in the eleventh month, the armistice was signed and the war came to an end. My father took great delight in reporting that Uncle Gerald served in the US Army until November 26th in 1918, when he received an honorable discharge along with $18.75 in travel pay for his twenty-one days of service. Upon his discharge from the Army, it was noted that Uncle Gerald was discharged from the US Army in excellent health and it was noted he served his entire enlistment on the UC campus.

My Brother, Mike

NATURE OR NURTURE? Many of us go through life wondering what makes us the people we are or the people we become. Is it the blueprint of life, DNA (our genetic code), and family heritage and ancestors that makes us the people we become? Or is it the environment we are raised in and live in, our family, friends, opportunities and education that makes us who we are.

Michael Joseph Mullany – Mike – was born in San Francisco in 1941, the year the United States entered World War II. Mike was the first son and there were three older sisters (Ann, Maureen and Lucille) in the family when he was born. The Irish naming convention was to name the first son after the father's father or the paternal grandfather. Our father, James Mullany, was the son of Michael and Julia Mullany. None of us in the family knew Michael or Julia because they died before any of us were born.

I was born four years later in 1941, just a few months before the end of World War II. I was given the name of James Leo; my father and maternal grandfather were named James, so I suspect I was named for both of them. My father had a brother named Leo, so my middle name was after him. My dad always told me he did not want me to be a junior, so he gave me a different middle name than his own. I always suspected that due to the spread in ages between my oldest sister and me that I may have been an "accident." In terms of nurture, my brother and I lived pretty much identical early lives. We were both born in Saint Mary's Hospital in San Francisco and spent our entire childhood in the same house on 19th Avenue in San Francisco and for a time even shared a bedroom. In terms of education we were both Catholics and attended St. Cecilia's Grammar School and Archbishop Riordan High School. Even our recreational pursuits were much the same, we both played the same Catholic Youth Organization (CYO) sports in grammar school. In high school, we both ran track and cross country, although I played basketball throughout high school. Also, like most Mullany's, neither of us were mechanically or musically inclined.

So, the question is: Why were we so different? Our basic nature and personalities were totally opposite. Although we were the same sex, and children number four and five in the birth order of the siblings, we were not particularly close as brothers or as young people. Mike was outgoing, he always wanted to be the center of attention, life of the party, telling jokes and being the funny guy with his friends, always trying to be noticed and paid attention to. For a time, he even resembled Jerry Lewis as top comic in the 1950s.

I was the total opposite; I was quiet and shy, never wanting to be noticed inside or outside of the family. I think it was my basic nature to be invisible, but being the youngest in a family of world class loud talkers – it was very easy for me to go unnoticed. I loved to go to my room and read books or newspapers. A hobby of mine was keeping score cards of baseball and basketball games I listened to on the radio. Because football did not have a scorekeeping system, I invented my own. It was a running shorthand scorecard of plays. I was not sure I could be called a loner as I did have friends, but when I was home, I preferred being alone with all my score books. I managed to avoid the ongoing loud chaos of a large family of talkers. I had nothing to say to my older siblings and my impression was that even if I did, they were not interested in hearing from "Little Jimmy's life."

The earliest incidence in our lives as brothers happened when I was in the infant-toddler stage. I have no memory of it, so I have only heard of this event from family members. It was a Sunday and my mother was at church and my father was not at home either. He may have been fishing or at the beach. Mike apparently was playing with matches under an inside staircase of our home and he started a fire. The fire department was called and put out the small blaze. My mother returned home to see the commotion with the firemen and truck at our house. My mother screamed, "Where's Jimmy?" The legend was my brother looked at her as if to say, "Jimmy? Who's Jimmy?" It turned out I was safe and the damage to the house was minor. The question at the time was, had the fire been just an accident of a boy playing with matches or was Mike so jealous of "Little Jimmy" that he was trying to burn the house down? I think the conclusion was it was just an accident, but in later years I wondered.

As we grew up and entered our school years, four years was such a gap I don't think we had much interaction. Mike was the "big kid" and he had his friends and did his own thing. I cannot recall that we played or interacted that much together until the years when I was in the fifth or sixth grade and Mike was in his early years of high school. The only exception was when our father took us to Mussel Rock Beach south of San Francisco. We invented games and played with each other as our father dozed on the beach.

Somewhere along the line, Mike became the dominating big brother. He was just bigger, stronger and older than me, so I did what he said. Most of our interactions were what I would call typical big brother-little brother stuff. Although we sometimes wrestled, it was mainly an opportunity for him to "beat me up." He was not really a dominating fighter, so mostly I would just give up without much damage being done. The one area where he could hurt me was with what was called the "Indian burn." This was when you were grabbed by the wrist with two hands twisting hard in opposite directions, creating a burn and leaving you with a red mark. He was pretty adept at this move.

I recall I regularly made his "goodie" run up to the store for snacks like candy, soda and chips. I think at one time I was a bit gullible, as he timed me once up and back to the store. After that he told me "I could break my record" by making fast trips for him. Another time, I think I was in the sixth or seventh grade and he made me make a second trick-or-treat run in our neighborhood just to get him candy. I felt that I paid him back slightly when on my second round some adults recognized me. I told them I was doing it because my brother made me do it because he was in high school. For some reason, I recall most people thought this was funny.

As we got older, Mike became something of the star of the family, although he later confided in me that *he* wanted center stage and my father was very hard to get off the stage. Dad was funny, weird, quirky, outspoken and opinionated. He was just a flat-out character. Mike was always trying to be funnier than Dad, but Dad seemed to have more attention-grabbing routines than Mike did. I personally thought in some odd way they were both competing for the attention of my mother, although my mother at times said Dad's true love in life was his twin brother, our Uncle Eddie. Mike had quite a temper and at times he would fly off the handle, and that was one of the things that I would fear of him.

I was something of a sickly child in that I had asthma at a young age, and cold would just wipe me out more than any other illnesses. So, when I was sick, I would miss school and would pretty much remain in my bed. Mike thought I was good comedy routine material so he would make me a regular butt of his jokes with his friends. Most of the jokes had to do with me being sick or spending a lot of time in bed. The jokes were not funny to me and in fact I thought they were mean-spirited. Also, because I had a large head, he thought it was funny to call me "Major Domo" (dome meaning head). I hated these jokes and never could figure out why being mean to me was less important than getting a laugh from his friends. This was another reason I kept my distance from him and was glad when he was not around.

 It was interesting with parents back then in the 1950s. They were the opposite of the helicopter parents of today. Most of the parents of our time that I knew were what I would call "the hands-off parents". For most parents back then, they wanted kids out of the house and not under foot. Dads focused on working and earning money to support the family, and stay-at-home moms generally ran the house and supervised the kids. Also, they let teachers and coaches manage the kids away from the home and unless notified of some problem, they let kids alone outside of the house. So, kids had lots of freedom outside of the home with little influence from their parents or adult supervision. Because my parents would make me nervous when they watched me play sports, I was happy that they did not attend my games, but my brother, who was more of a performer, wanted his parents to watch his sports competition. In either case, because my dad worked and my mom did not drive, they seldom attended our sporting events. My brother became a star outside of the home when he achieved success as a runner in cross-country and track at Riordan High School. So, in a way he became his own PR man and I think that made him a favorite in the house, especially with my mom. But neither of our parents were big on patting us on the back or praising us for our athletic or academic success.

 It was not all bad growing up with Mike, and some of the best childhood memories are the times we went together on trips with our dad. It seemed when Mike and I were together without his friends or others he wanted to impress, we could have fun. A couple of car trips to Southern California with just my dad,

Mike and me are really memorable. Mike was a fifteen-year-old unlicensed driver when Dad handed over the steering wheel to him about three blocks from our home, telling Mike, "You can drive the rest of the way." All the way to LA with an unlicensed driver? This was not as unusual as it sounds, as we later found out my father also was unlicensed. Shortly after turning the driving duties over to Mike, my dad would promptly fall asleep. On one of those trips, I had assumed my usual spot in the back seat with my pillow propped up against the door. I went to straighten the pillow out and opened the back door by accident. (The back doors in our old Dodge opened in the opposite way than the front doors), So my back door whooshed open with me holding onto to the handle for dear life. Pops was dozing next to Mike in the front bench seat and Mike rousted him up by saying, "I think Jim is falling out of the car." Pops ordered Mike to pull over before I fell out.

    The centerpiece of those visits was the stop in downtown Los Angeles where our eccentric Uncle Gerald lived in a residential hotel, The San Carlos Hotel. We would stay at the San Carlos and were always the only kids ever allowed to stay there. Because Uncle Gerald was a notorious pack rat-hoarder, no one except my father was ever allowed to enter his room. So, the usual scene in our room would be Gerald coming to visit us so he could talk with my dad. As a lifelong childless bachelor, he was not fond of kids, nor did he care to have them in his presence when he was telling stories. The typical scene went like this: Gerald would start telling one of his stories to Dad in a loud voice (as he was hard of hearing) while Mike and I would try to watch the TV in the same room. The louder Uncle Gerald talked, the higher Mike would turn up the TV volume so we could hear. Without a word, Gerald would go to the TV and turn down the volume. This would go on a few times, and my father would issue the order for us to go out and play or give us bus tokens or money to get rid of us.

In a residential hotel of old people, the only play we could come up with was riding the elevator. But we did not fully understand the concept of the manual elevator that needed an operator. So, whenever we found the elevator empty, Mike would take us for a ride. Of course, when the operator came back and his elevator was gone, after a few hikes up and down stairs to retrieve his elevator, we were forbidden to use the elevator without the operator present. Also, there was a cleaner's shop on the ground floor within the hotel's street front, and much to the chagrin of the workers there, Mike and I managed to emerge from behind their front counter. How we made it to the back of a cleaner's shop down the street from the lobby of the San Carlos Hotel was a bit of a mystery to us.

Because Gerald and my dad were annoyed to have us around the hotel, Dad would send off us off on our own for adventuresome bus trips to ball games and Universal Studios. Although we were well versed in riding buses and street cars in San Francisco, we had not an idea about the LA bus system and its system of tokens. We both recall our dad giving us bus tokens and just putting us on a bus to find our own way to Gilmore Field in Hollywood, the home of the Hollywood Stars Pacific Coast League baseball club. When the bus reached the end of the line, we were told by the bus driver we were nowhere near the field and at fifteen and eleven years old, we had to make our own way on foot to the park miles away, through some very questionable neighborhoods. Of course, we did not have a way to reach my dad or Gerald's hotel.

I entered Riordan High School in the fall of 1959, the same year my brother had graduated the previous spring. But I literally chose to follow in his footsteps when I choose to run cross-country and track. I started out wearing the red Adidas running flats he had worn. Mike had become something of a track legend at Riordan, setting records in the mile and also helping lead the team to some league championships. At times, I felt the disappointment of those who had coached and run with Mike, expecting me to match his glory or his personality. Although I periodically won races, it was not enough to those who knew Mike. It was only when all those guys who knew Mike had graduated that I felt I was freed from his shadow. In a peculiar way it had not really bothered me that much, as I gained a little recognition and social connections from being Mike's brother that I would not otherwise have had.

One event in the summer when I was heading into my senior year of high school still haunts me about my brother and our relationship. Mike attended the University of New Mexico on a track scholarship and he would come home during the summer. That particular summer I was training very hard for my upcoming cross-country season, as I had a chance to be the number one runner on the team. Mike usually would not train most of the summer, until about the last month. He smoked during the summer, went to parties with his friends and sometimes worked at a summer job. Training was not a priority to him. Late in the summer, one day he asked me to go on a training run with him at Ocean Beach in San Francisco. We ran for about five or six miles at a good pace, but because I was in running shape and he was not, he struggled to keep up with me and at one point, gasping for breath, he told me to keep running as he could not keep up with my pace. Afterward, he said we had to have a match race in the next two weeks around Lake Merced, which was about a five-mile run. I told him I knew he could beat me when he was in shape so there was no point to having a race. I think he was a bit humiliated that I had beaten him on this run, so he wanted to humiliate me. He even went so far as to tell some of his friends about it. Fortunately, the big race never happened.

My brother told me later in life that if he had been treated as poorly by his older brother as I had by him, it was likely he would choose to not have a relationship with that brother as an adult. I sometimes wonder why I did not have a relationship with him later on. I guess I did not like or could not deal with conflict or confrontations. He once told me he could not see ever us having a close relationship when we became adults, the inference being he (Mike) would prefer not to be friends with me as an adult and it would be his decision, not mine. This hurt me for a time and I never forgot it, although ironically, we have somehow managed to remain friends over the years and are still talking to each other well into our seventies.

Mike – High School, 1959

Jim – Grammar School, 1959

Jim and Mike, 2015

March 1998
With San Francisco 49er greats
Dwight Clark and Joe Montana —
in commemoration of "The Catch."

JOYS IN LIFE

(To my grandchildren) "I may not be the most important person in your life, I just hope when you hear my name you will smile and think 'that's my Poppa'."
Jim Mullany

OUR DOGS

*"Handle every stressful situation like a dog.
If you can't eat it or play with it, just pee on it and walk away."*
Unknown

Lady – Our Perfect Pet

Growing up in San Francisco, I never had a pet during my childhood. Reflecting back on those days in the 1950s in San Francisco, I now realize that none of my friends or relatives had pets either. Oh, our neighborhood has the "crazy cat lady" as we called her, who seemed to have had more than enough cats for all the families in the Parkside District. I think for a time I actually believed her name was "crazy cat lady" because that is what everyone called her.

Because my friends and neighbors did not have pets, I do not recall thinking very much about having a pet. I was the youngest of five children, with an age spread of about fifteen years, so by the time I came along, the topic of pets had been exhausted and no explanation was ever offered to me. I can vaguely recall my father saying that he had too many mouths to feed to have a pet, but I think there may have been other reasons. Neither of my parents had a pet growing up, and they did not indicate any affection towards animals. Another factor in my petless life was the reality that San Francisco was not very pet-friendly during my youth. It was busy with traffic, a congested urban area with tiny yards. Because none of my friends or relatives had a pet, I never felt deprived for not having a cat or dog. Lassie, Rin Tin Tin, Roy Roger's dog Bullet and other fictional television dogs were all the pets I needed back then.

My firsthand experience with pets did not begin until I had children of my own. First, there was Daisy the cat, who was something of a pet in training for my little girls. One evening when I could barely breathe and my eyes had just about swollen shut during Daisy's initial stay in our house, I realized that cats were not going to work in our home. Daisy's exile was clinched when she developed the habit of urinating in the laundry basket and on our breakfast room window.

Once the girls started school when we had moved to Sacramento, the pet of choice was a small white rat named Ratty. When my eyes started to water and sneezing bouts ensued, at first, I did not connect these symptoms with Ratty. But a visit to an allergist confirmed that rats gave off a similar dander as cats. I recall informing my young daughter, Adrienne, that it might come down to Daddy or Ratty in our home. Her sad eyes and silent response reminded me of the famous Jack Benny routine. The noted skinflint Benny was confronted by a robber in a dark alley, who demanded "Your money or your life!" After a long silent pause, Benny responded, "I'm thinking, I'm thinking."

After Ratty it was Noelle the hamster, who actually turned out to be Noel, and we nicknamed him Hammy. Hammy proved to be a prized pet in that his size and demeanor was perfect for two little girls, and his lack of cat-rat secretions was much prized by me.

But Ratty and Hammy just proved to be warm-up acts or the preliminary pet performers for the star attraction pet in our family's life – Lady, the perfect dog. Lady came into our lives as a stray dog that was found wandering in a local park by an acquaintance of my wife. After doing everything possible to locate the dog's owners, the friend called my wife and said he had "the perfect dog" for our family. He said his first choice would have been to keep the dog for his own family, but with a young child and another dog that wasn't possible. He said that this well-cared-for and trained dog would be perfect for our family.

We named her Lady because she reminded us of the fictional Lady from *The Lady and the Tramp* story. She was a small dog, weighing about fifteen pounds, who was predominantly black with light brown feet, snout, and eyebrows. She was estimated to be about two years old and looked to be part cocker spaniel with possibly some terrier in her. She was everything you would want in a pet – a loyal companion, smart, affectionate, and gentle with the girls, and for the next fourteen years, she was an integral part of our family. We may have disagreed about some things over those years, but we were unanimous in our love for Lady.

I am not sure what characteristics or qualities dogs have that enable them to worm their way into our hearts and become valued members of the family. Lady just seemed to want to please and be part of all our family activities. The look in her brown eyes sent a message that we were valued, important and worthy of her loyalty. She always looked so eager to hear our next pronouncements as if we were always on the brink of doing or saying something momentous or noteworthy. Like most dogs, she was a good listener and seemed to hang on our every word no matter how silly or meaningless it might be.

Lady was quick, agile and gentle as she moved around our house and yard, always seeming to avoid obstacles or dangers in her path. We had noted her speed and endurance, so she joined me as a running partner in some doggie dash footraces in the Sacramento area. I recall with a bit of pride the day we approached the finish line in a three-mile run, and a young spectator yelled out to us, "Way to go, I think you are first in the big man, little dog division." A dream come true – first in the big man, little dog division. Our reward was a forty-pound bag of dog food.

Her one weakness was her habit of chasing cats and sometimes not being able to distinguish cats from other small furry creatures. She once pulled a back muscle during a particularly spirited cat-chasing effort. The vet who treated her commented that the injury might qualify Lady for canine worker's compensation. Another time, in the middle of the night Lady's "cat chase" was actually an encounter with a skunk that Lady announced by rubbing against beds, couches, and carpets before we could corner her for removal to the garage.

But rather than her glories or setbacks, what marked Lady as special was her day-to-day presence in our lives: her full body tail-wagging greetings; her presence at our triumphs and our tears; her joyous speedy romps around our house to display her pleasure with our attention; her curling up to us for warmth on cold winter evenings. Somehow, she managed to bring out the best in us over those fourteen years, and for that, we will be forever grateful for her significant role in our lives.

Pepper

"I know you are going to be mad at me," my wife told me over the telephone. I still vividly recall receiving this call at my office following a Christmas luncheon back in the 1980s. She went on to explain that she had taken in the neighborhood stray dog that we had seen roaming our suburban Sacramento neighborhood. She told me that the sight of the dog, laying on the sidewalk with his black shaggy coat covered with a layer of frost that morning, was more than her heart could bear. She felt she needed to warn me of his presence in our home before I arrived later that day. She reassured me that his stay at our house would be temporary until we could find a good home for him.

When I arrived home later that day, my anger quickly dissolved when faced with this dog. He looked at me with his big brown eyes that were both sad and hopeful. His look said that I was his last hope, the end of the road, and if not me then there would be no one left to save him. You see, I was the sole male living in a household of females, with a wife, two young daughters, and even a female dog named Lady. The homeless dog we came to name Pepper had a look that spoke directly to me. It said, "I may not be much to look at, I may not be smart or well-trained, but I am a guy, and maybe we could be pals if you will just give me a chance." He had me right there with that look. I suspect this was the scenario my wife and daughters had imagined all along.

Lady was the perfect dog everyone loved. She was a small dog of predominantly cocker spaniel lineage, well-mannered, refined, classy, a summa cum laude graduate of obedience school. Pepper was not. Pepper was the classic street dog. His black fur was shaggy and unkempt. His long snout was lined with some salt-colored graying fur. His lineage was undistinguished and indeterminant. But hidden within the rough and ordinary exterior of Pepper's appearance there was personality, character, and a spirit that had allowed him to survive on the street.

My first trip to the vet with Pepper was the first of many adventures I would experience with this free-spirited canine. While we patiently waited in line at the front counter, I happened to glance down at Pepper just when he lifted his leg and proceeded to pee on the leg of a lady in front of me in line. I was horrified, for nothing in my background, education or life experiences had provided me with the proper words of apology to a stranger who had just had her pant leg whizzed with dog urine. As the idea of slinking away and fleeing the scene flashed through my mind, I noticed some of the people waiting behind me in line were chuckling and snickering. Pepper had just made their day. I tapped the woman on the shoulder and embarrassingly informed her that my dog had just unleashed a steady stream on her leg. She glanced down, smiled at Pepper, and said, "Honey, in my life they have done a lot worse to me." With relief, I pulled Pepper away to a corner of the lobby, only to be confronted with him then peeing on the beautiful pet product display. Thus started my life with Pepper.

When growing up as a member of a large family with five kids, I had not had the opportunity to have a pet because, as my father always said, "there were too many mouths to feed in our family." Pepper was my first dog, so I guess I could say our relationship was a boy and his dog, forty years delayed. Pepper would provide many challenges to my patience and friendship, but his good nature, his easygoing innocence with his "did I do something wrong" look, and his fierce protectiveness of us all, helped forge and cement the bond of friendship between us.

Pepper was an escape artist, but his escapes were neither malicious nor intended as runaway breakouts. It was just his nature to be part of the action, whether it be the lure of another dog strolling in the front yard or the desire to join the fun with a group of kids. His usual method of escape was using a stack of firewood in the side yard as a launching pad to propel himself over our six-foot fence. He left his mark on that fence, as tufts of his fur were permanently embedded at the top of the fence where he had often scraped the top during his leaps.

Years after he joined our family, the end for Pepper came much as it had begun. A fierce February storm, a wind-blown fence, a final curious escape, a speeding car – a hit and run. When found by a neighbor in the evening darkness, he was laying in the street and a layer of frost had begun to cover his coat. I had lost a friend. Our family mourned.

My 18 seconds of fame with Joe Montana

THE GIFT –
MY 18 SECONDS WITH JOE MONTANA

I know that my essay about a special gift should be noble, inspiring, life-changing, miraculous and giving. I suspect that many writers would take one of these approaches and their writings would be heartfelt, emotional and educational. This essay will not be one of those. For my story of a gift is one of the more selfish variety, a guilty pleasure, one of getting what you want rather than what you need. In fact, to ensure that this gift was the right one, it is one I had to resort to giving myself.

Growing up in San Francisco, from a very young age I had followed the fortunes and misfortunes of the San Francisco 49ers football team with a passion that bordered on fanaticism. Like many passions in life, this one defied logic or objective analysis – I lived and died with this team from childhood through adolescence into middle age and beyond. Over the years and decades, I had followed the team up until the 1980s, and I came to expect that they would usually find creative and innovative ways to lose football games. The rallying cry for the 49er Faithful over the years came to be a resigned "Wait Until Next Year," as we generally accepted the fact that good things would seldom happen to them this year. I think it was more than coincidental that in the early years, the mascot of the team was a wild, drunken miner. The team's logo showed this character whooping it up with a six-shooter in one hand and a bottle of whiskey in the other. This definitely would be politically incorrect for San Francisco these days. The miner's real-life counterpart at the games was a scraggly and scrawny looking bearded man in a moth-eaten red jacket who rode an old burro named Clementine. Neither the burro nor the team seemed to go anywhere.

All this changed for the team in the early 1980s when, quite suddenly and unexpectedly, the team became winners, and most San Francisco sports fans caught a serious case of 49er Fever. Heading up the heroics of the team was a hero whose name seemed to be a perfect fit for a western hero – Joe Montana. Montana had become a genuine sports legend before our very eyes, and to 49ers fans, he became the most popular person in San Francisco. No matter how bleak or disastrous things looked for the 49ers, more times than not Joe Cool saved the day to snatch a last minute, come-from-behind victory.

One day I was reading the Sacramento Bee's sports page when a small advertisement in the corner of the page caught my attention. The ad announced that Joe Montana would be making a special appearance at a Sacramento sports memorabilia shop, and for the princely sum of $300, a framed painting of the sports icon could be purchased. But what really caught my attention was that the ad mentioned that each purchaser would be able to meet Montana and have a photo taken with the legend. Here I was, an adult man with a family, but all logic and common sense went out the window with the thought of meeting Joe Montana, a 49er hero. I was a kid again, and the thing that closed the deal in my mind was when the ad mentioned this would be a perfect Father's Day gift, as Montana would be appearing the day after Father's Day.

My strategy and approach were as transparent and obvious as the punchline of a joke told by a third-rate comedian. One evening at dinner, I casually mentioned to my wife and daughters that I knew what I wanted as a gift for Father's Day. Because my usual Father's Day gifts were some handmade cards and a special meal of my favorite foods, I received some quizzical looks. After explaining my idea of the Montana meeting to them, my wife, true to her CPA profession, cut directly to the bottom line as she asked, "How much?" I informed her of the bargain price of $300. She made a generous gesture by informing our daughters that this would be something that would make their dad very happy, and thereby the deal was sealed.

On the June evening when the big day came, I joined a group of about 200 or 300 poor souls like myself. I noticed some had even brought props, like young children and elderly parents, to deflect attention from the fact that this was really all about grown men acting like children. I had not seen such a motley gathering since the last police sting operation had been broadcast on the local news.

The written and verbal instructions we received prior to meeting Joe were ones befitting meeting royalty. We would be granted a maximum of 18 seconds in which we would shake Joe's hand, pose for the picture, and impart a message to him. We were jokingly told that although he had injured his right arm he was still a football player, so we should be sure to exchange a firm handshake with him but not attempt a bone crusher or a dead fish grip.

As I approached the curtain for my personal audience with Joe, I expected that behind the curtain an elaborate practical joke of Oz proportions awaited me. But there was Montana and my reluctantly departing predecessor fan who was saying, "But Joe, I think you still owe me four seconds."

I was prepared for my 18 seconds. Knowing that Joe was a father of four children I threw him off guard by asking him how his Father's Day was. No chitchat about his greatness or my greatest Montana memory from me. Joe said his Father's Day was great and asked me about my own. Knowing the clock was ticking, I quickly told him that mine was very good too, and my daughter had gifted me with the very shirt I was wearing. I said it would impress her greatly if I got "Joe Montana's personal review" of her selection. He said laughingly, "Tell her Joe Montana says it is a great shirt." And thus ended my 18-second encounter with greatness.

The next day I was kidded by co-workers who had learned that I had paid out a princely sum to meet the legend. And the ribbing grew more potent when they learned of the 18-second limitation of my encounter. I silenced all with my retort, "But those were 18 high quality and very meaningful seconds."

The Rolling Pin

In January of 1995, the last rites of our marriage were being conducted at our kitchen table in Citrus Heights, California. Bonnie, my wife of twenty-seven years, was moving out and she was packing away some kitchen utensils in a cardboard box. I was numb, thinking that my lifetime partner and best friend had made the decision to end our marriage.

I always had the belief that our marriage was forever and that we would grow old together. We had dated for three years in the mid-1960s when we were in our late teens and early twenties and had married in 1968. To an outsider, our marriage may have succumbed to the "empty nest" syndrome now that our two daughters were in college and for all practical purposes had moved out of our home. That may have been part of the story, but it was more complicated than that — we were no longer the same people we had been in our twenties now that we were in our fifties, and we had grown apart. We had moved in different directions.

I think it was appropriate or ironic that the end of our marriage was being played out in the kitchen of our home because as my father had once proclaimed, ours was a marriage made in heaven because "Bonnie loved to cook and Jim loved to eat." This had been especially true for the many years I was a long-distance runner and seemed to have a bottomless pit for food, especially the baked goods that Bonnie was particularly adept at preparing. Cakes, pies and homemade bread were my favorites, and Bonnie seemed particularly skillful and creative in these areas. So, I guess you could say we were co-dependents when it came to food.

As Bonnie pulled out the various kitchen utensils and implements, I was barely aware of what they were and what function they performed. But then she pulled out a rolling pin and started to put it into the box. I protested, "You are not taking that rolling pin, are you?" I need to say at this point that this was not any ordinary rolling pin, but it was something like the Stradivarius of rolling pins. The rolling pin was a very old solid wood rolling pin, and Bonnie had made good use of that rolling pin over the years.

Bonnie responded with surprise to my protest about the rolling pin. "How often have you used this rolling pin since we've had it?" I told I had never touched the rolling pin, but now she was moving out of the house, I might take up baking in the future. The absurdity of this statement struck both of us almost before the words had left my mouth. The seriousness of the moment was broken and we both burst out laughing. Bonnie then dug deeper into the drawer and pulled out the plastic K-Mart version of a rolling pin that almost looked like a toy in comparison to the solid wood one. She told me in a gently sarcastic tone that here was the rolling pin that I could keep to use when I start my baking career. The rolling pin had served to diffuse what could have been a very tense and volatile situation.

Now, years later, Bonnie and I remain friends, as we have chosen to focus our relationship on those things we share that are good and positive – our daughters, our three wonderful grandchildren, and some delicious butter horn rolls which are the product of an old rolling pin.

And my baking career? It is still on hold.

*Point Pinos Lighthouse
in Pacific Grove*

COMFORT ZONES – MOVING TO PACIFIC GROVE

My life, like many others, is filled with comfort zones, those places that are familiar, predictable, easy and habitual. These comfort zones are filled with people, places and things that are like the word comfort, they are soothing, easy, free of pain and fear. But comfort zones can also mean dull, routine, safe, boring, and lacking in challenges or stimulation. For some, getting out of one's comfort zone may mean jumping out of airplanes, walking down the dark alleys of life, or having the courage to take that small baby step into a world that is unfamiliar, scary, or just unknown.

I am learning, as I get older, that comfort zones offer something of a contradiction in my life. At times, I find it easier to retreat into comfortable, safe and familiar places of habit, while at the same time feel an urgent call to stretch and challenge myself with new experiences as the sands of time rush through the hourglass of my life. At this point in my life, who really cares if I fail or fall flat on my face trying to master a new skill or venture into the unknown? I have come to think of my 2008 mantra as, "It is better to have tried and failed than to have never tried."

It had been something of a dream of mine that when I retired I would move to Pacific Grove. For as long as I can remember, going back to the late 1950s, I had loved visiting Butterfly Town, even before it was called Butterfly Town.

But in many lives, including mine, there was a gap between my dreams and my reality. It was funny how different they usually were. When I retired after about thirty years living in Sacramento, the opportunity to move to Pacific Grove confronted me. It was now or never time. It was going to be a challenge for me because I was going to be moving to an area where I did not know a living soul. There would be no safety net of family and friends and familiar haunts to lean on. It was strange that the deciding factor in my decision was reading a news article profiling a young actor. The actor mentioned how his career had floundered until he made the decision to move to a new area where he did not know anyone. He said the move was one of the most exciting and challenging things he had done in his young life, but he believed that the creativity of his acting and his growth as a person demanded such a bold move.

    The move from Sacramento to Pacific Grove was accomplished with little fanfare or trouble. As I made this transition, I found myself often thinking in clichés: today is the first day of the rest of your life; every day is a gift, that is why it is called the present; time to stop and smell the roses; just do it; life is short, so live for today. Another one I was reminded of by a friend was when I told her the cost of rental housing in Pacific Grove: your dreams do not come cheap.

    In coming to the beautiful Central Coast, it has been as if the entire world has made a quarter turn and everything has changed. The steamy central valley of the summer has become the chilly, fog-enshrouded central coast; the view of the Sierra Nevada Mountains in the distance has become the crashing surf of the Pacific Ocean on my doorstep; the blare of rush hour traffic on Interstate 80 has become the cacophony of gulls and crows, with the steady harmony of ocean waves lapping on the rocks and sandy beaches. Rather than waves of people in cars, there are the waves of the ocean. A shifting scene of fresh smells and salty air that produces a calmness contrasts greatly with the frantic pace of the city. The sea just seems to wash away any tension or stress one might have, and the waves can be mesmerizing.

    Living on the coast, I have learned to take the time to really see and hear things that I encounter every day in a way that I did not know how to do in the city. Every day is a gift, and I have learned to appreciate the small things: a mother deer hopping my back fence while her young offspring tries to figure out what to do can be a lesson to them and me; a stop for traffic at an intersection on Ocean View can reveal the waterspout of a humpback whale in the distance; I have learned that I need to be ready and receptive to these sights and sounds that abound in my new home.

Life is short, but there are times when days can be long. Sometimes the difference between the exquisite feeling of solitude and the barren landscape of loneliness can be slight. To sit quietly and hear the silence of nature can be either a revelation or it can be a lonely period of sadness. I am learning that the key is learning to distinguish between these two conditions as I expand my comfort zone every day. This chapter of my life is still being written each day, but like a good book, it has turned out to be a real page-turner.

Beautiful Pacific Grove

*Author Jim Mullany with his family,
2018 in Pacific Grove, CA*

LIFE HAPPENS

*"Life is what happens to you
while you're busy making other plans"*
Allen Saunders

Learning to Say Yes to Life

The wedding invitation arrived in late 1993, announcing the wedding of my nephew Jerry Regan to be held in New Orleans on a weekend in March of 1994. Jerry was one of my sister Ann's five children. The family had moved from the San Francisco Bay Area to Wichita, Kansas in the mid-1970s due to a job transfer for husband Patrick. My initial reaction to the invitation was typical for me back then: sorry, I do not have enough time, enough money, or enough motivation to inconvenience myself to break from my regular routine. At the time, I was just approaching my fiftieth birthday and was living in Sacramento with two daughters who were nearing college age; going to this wedding seemed to be a luxury that I was neither able nor willing to afford.

But something highly extraordinary and unusual occurred in that my brother Mike and my wife Bonnie both encouraged and recommended that I attend the wedding, and over time they wore down my resistance to the idea. The extraordinary thing was that my brother and my wife never agreed on anything and were always at odds; not only were they never on the same page, they were apparently never even reading from the same book. I took their separate encouragements as a sign that this event was something that I should make an effort to attend. Their reasons for me to make this trip were: a chance to renew family relationships; an event that comes only once and will be gone; a fun trip; a time to just get away and experience something different and new. All must have struck a chord with me because I did go to New Orleans for that weekend in March 1994.

Upon arrival in New Orleans, I learned of another sign that this weekend was special, or just meant to be. The annual St. Patrick's Day Parade and celebration were being held in New Orleans that weekend. Our family of Irish-Americans was filled with people named Maloney, Mullany, Devine, and Regan, which further reinforced my belief that New Orleans was the place where we were meant to be for that weekend. Our family filled a rambling bed and breakfast home named the Park View in the Garden District on historic St. Charles Avenue, directly across from Tulane University and close to Loyola University and the Sacred Heart Church where Jerry and Grace were to be married on Saturday afternoon. All this contributed to a weekend to be remembered.

We filled the weekend with family time of stories, catching up with news amid lots of laughter and even some tears as we Irish are wont to do, as we remembered family members no longer around to share these times with us, and how in a small way it was a tribute to our deceased parents that we were united for a family wedding on St. Patrick's Day weekend. It was a New Orleans weekend with the parade, trips along the Mississippi River, and excursions to the French Quarter, Bourbon Street and far too much good food and good drink, if that is possible. With too much time at Pat O'Brien's bar, some of us almost missed the wedding due to the power of Hurricanes, not the natural storms that periodically hit the Gulf Coast, but the potent drink Pat O'Brien's is known for. How fitting for an Irish family.

For those of us who attended, we talked about that weekend for days, weeks, months and years across the miles of our widely-scattered lives. A weekend had provided us with a lifetime of memories, a time of life not to have been missed.

That wedding invitation is one I have thought of many times over the years for the changes it awakened in my life. After that weekend, I made it a point in the future to not to miss family weddings, birthdays, and anniversary parties, because I came to recognize them as "once in a lifetime" opportunities rather than inconveniences to my routine, which reminds me of the saying that life happens while you are planning for other things.

So now all of those invitations that I receive for travel across the world, for adventures near and far and for life itself, are more likely met these days with a resounding and enthusiastic RSVP of – Yes, I will be attending! Yes, I can be bothered! Yes, I can be inconvenienced! Yes, I can experience the fullness of life!

Changes In My Life

My wife Bonnie and I had been married for over nine years in late 1977, and in those nine years, we had experienced some changes along the way. First and most importantly, there were our two children, our daughter Erin, who had been born in 1973, and our youngest daughter Adrienne, who was a "bicentennial baby" born in 1976. We had moved a few times, first of all because of my hitch in the US Air Force; we had lived six months in Texas and three years on the edge of the Mojave Desert in Redlands, California. I had avoided serving overseas unless you count Texas, which was something of a foreign assignment to us Californians. Our idea and plan were to spend the rest of our lives in the San Francisco Bay Area once I was discharged from the service. It was the place where most of our families and friends resided, and we both loved San Francisco and our home in Pacifica, a seaside suburb of San Francisco. But we were both smart enough to never say never about moving from the Bay Area.

In late 1977, my employer, the Investigative Unit of the Employment Development, had a major reorganization; the staff was told that we would have to be prepared to quickly make decisions for possible relocations and promotions. We submitted our wish lists of assignments, and my top three were all Bay Area locations, with my assignment in San Francisco as my top choice and Santa Rosa and San Jose my second and third choices. When the day of decision arrived, we were told to be at our desks and prepared to make quick decisions, as the offers would be fluid and we would have only one opportunity to make our choices. I was first comforted by the fact that my decision would be no decision – I would remain in San Francisco and continue with my same Special Investigator assignment.

But two days later, everything changed. I was informed that a man who had selected Sacramento had changed his mind and he declined the Sacramento position. I was informed that the choice was now mine and it included a significant promotion, full moving expenses paid by the state, and a new assignment to the prestigious four-person internal investigation unit. I had until the end of the day to make my final decision. I called Bonnie, and I think we were both surprised that we quickly made the same decision – take the job. Our family was ready for a change and the challenge, as we realized we had pretty much gone as far as we could go in the high cost of living San Francisco Bay Area. For our family to grow and progress, we needed to make changes, and we agreed this was our opportunity. I informed our deputy director at the end of the day, and the job was mine. My wife and I later laughed about our decision, as neither of us had ever been to Sacramento.

The changes we encountered in our move from San Francisco Bay Area to Sacramento paled in comparison to those of immigrants and refugees who move or escape threats of violence to a culture that is worlds apart from their own and have to start their lives over from the bottom. However, the move from San Francisco to Sacramento did mean changes, because:

San Francisco was cool - Sacramento was hot;
San Francisco was urban - Sacramento was suburban;
San Francisco was "The City" - Sacramento was "The State";
San Francisco was vertical - Sacramento was horizontal;
San Francisco was row houses - Sacramento was ranch houses on acreage;
San Francisco was a world-class cosmopolitan city - Sacramento was Middle America;
San Francisco was seafood and sourdough - Sacramento was tomatoes, rice, and almonds;
San Francisco was concrete, glass, and stucco - Sacramento was oaks and pines;
San Francisco was oceans and bays - Sacramento was rivers and lakes;
San Francisco was ocean winds - Sacramento was delta breezes;

Sacramento was summer colds and sweatshirts - Sacramento was spring allergies, T-shirts, and tank tops;

San Francisco was the marine layer and ocean fogs in the summer - Sacramento was Tule fog in the winter;

San Francisco was the Giants and 49ers (and Warriors) - Sacramento was the Kings, the Hornets, and the Aggies;

But in the end, San Francisco and Sacramento were both places we would call "home".

Sacramento Tower Bridge

Epilogue

A few years after we moved to Sacramento, I left the investigation field to work for Social Services, and I helped to establish the state-wide transitional child care and in-house voluntary paternity programs, two programs that have helped millions of parents and families. Bonnie was at first a stay-at-home mom until our children reached middle school; then she returned to college at the age of forty to obtain her accounting degree, became a CPA, and established her own accounting firm.

Our children blossomed under the educational systems in Sacramento. Erin obtained a business degree from Sacramento State University, attended an exchange program at the University of London, and taught for two years in China. She is now married and the mother of Ian James and they live in the same home where she grew up. Adrienne obtained a degree in biological science from UC Davis and discovered that her best job opportunities would be in Silicon Valley, so she moved to San Jose and worked for a high-tech firm, and now is married with two children. Her husband is Vice President for Facebook. Sadly, Bonnie and I separated after twenty-seven years of marriage, but we remain connected to our children's families as Poppa and Grammy to our grandchildren.

We have never regretted our decision to make the move to Sacramento, and we lived with those changes for over thirty years. We still love San Francisco and the Bay Area, but we discovered we could also love Sacramento.

The Moment

My moment came in the early 1980s on the 16th-floor meeting room of a very ugly state office building in Sacramento, California in front of a three-person Department of Social Services interview panel. I was interviewing for a position of Associate Governmental Program Analyst (AGPA) in the Aid to Families with Dependent Children (AFDC) Policy Implementation Bureau (PIB) of the State Department of Social Services. It was my grand slam home run in the bottom of the ninth, my Super Bowl-winning touchdown, and my buzzer beater – a winning three-point shot swishing through the nets in an NBA finals moment. And in my head the words of actress Sally Field rattled around in my head: **"They like me, they like me, they really like me."**

But let me go back to the beginning of the story, all the way to June of 1968 in San Francisco when I began my State of California career. In June of 1968, my postgraduate degree in real life began on the streets of San Francisco following my graduation from San Francisco State College with an undergraduate degree in Sociology with an emphasis in Criminology. I think my real education began when I was hired as a Special Investigator trainee for the State Department of Employment in San Francisco's Coastal Region headquarters in downtown San Francisco. Although I had worked for four years at the Rincon Annex Post Office while attending college and was exposed to the full variety of San Francisco society, I believe that up until starting my job as an investigator I had lived something of a sheltered life. That sheltered life was quickly shattered when I was exposed to the real life of a fraud investigator working the "mean streets" of San Francisco. And take my word for it, beyond the tourist attractions and well-known sights of San Francisco there was a dark and dangerous underbelly of the city that greatly contrasted to bright lights and attractive well-known areas of San Francisco.

I worked with a seasoned, experienced crew of eight to ten investigators who had seen it all and done it all in their careers. Most were more than twenty years my senior, and almost to a man they had served in the military during a time of war or had years of investigative experience in police and governmental agencies. This was not a warm and fuzzy group that would remind one of the Barney Miller squad room in the popular TV series. But they did exhibit their own brand of dark humor, and I probably learned more about real life in the world than I had ever learned in the college classrooms.

I worked mainly fraud cases that involved scams, deceptions or outright thefts, but some of the suspects were actually creative and ingenious in their cons. Back in the late 1960s and 1970s, there was an informal code of honor among cons who committed fraud – they generally, but not always, limited their deviant behavior to acts they could commit with pen and paper and deception. This meant most of them were not involved in violent or assaultive crime. But on the edges of their fraud, there was other criminal behavior that brought us near the world of the Zebra and Zodiac killers and the Symbionese Liberation Army, best known for the kidnapping of newspaper heiress Patty Hearst and a Sacramento bank robbery that ended in the murder of a middle age woman who happened to be a customer at the time of the robbery. Some of the SLA members happened to also be involved in fraudulent, underground economy activity.

After investigating external fraud for more than ten years, interrupted by a four-year stint in the US Air Force, I received a promotion to Senior Special Investigator which included a transfer to Sacramento. I have never understood why government investigators like FBI agents are designated as "special," either as investigators or senior investigators. I never felt that I was "special." The new assignment in Sacramento was with a small elite squad assigned to internal fraud that was alleged to have been committed by Employment

Department employees. The crimes of embezzlement, extortion, harassment, and internal thefts were the crimes the internal investigators were called upon to investigate. Life was better for my family in Sacramento with two young daughters just starting or ready to start school. The quality of life in Sacramento was a major factor in our move.

    The working situation and conditions in this investigative squad were much different than my previous experience, as this job involved high profile allegations that often came in from the legislative hotline where citizens could notify their state legislator of allegations of wrong-doing by state employees. These investigations were of a highly sensitive nature and were to be conducted in an utmost confidential manner. This was necessary in order to protect the rights and privacy of employees, their supervision, and management. Although the job was highly prized, it provided no additional pay or benefits to the investigators who were required to travel throughout the state on very short notice and required long stretches of absences from home with some of the assignments also requiring long working hours. The long periods of absences from home caused strain on my family life and caused me to miss some significant and important events in my children's lives and put additional strain on my wife.

    After a few years of this, I realized the stress and pressures of this job were taking their toll on me both physically and mentally and were depriving our family of a "normal life." I wanted to move my career in a different direction. But except for my time as an accounting and finance clerk in the Air Force, my only work experience was as a "special investigator," and I no longer wanted to be an investigator. I felt trapped. I studied state job opening announcements to evaluate what positions my status as a journeyman investigator qualified me for so that I could make a lateral transfer. I felt there was nothing out there for me until I had a fortunate encounter with my neighbor, Gary. Gary was a successful business executive with the leading optical company in California. Gary told me that the unique skills that I had acquired and developed as an investigator would be attractive to an employer and in some instances exceeded those who might meet the basic job qualifications. So, I applied for a job as a state analyst with the Department of Social Services, and that was how I came to be in that ugly state building in front of that interview panel. And then they asked me "the question" that led to "the moment." "Why do you think your experience as an investigator qualifies you for this analyst job?"

And by the time I had finished my answer, I knew that I had the panel and that I had the job. Even though there were thirty or forty others applying for the job, I knew the job was mine and my moment had arrived.

An Unfinished Life Changes Overnight

The Wednesday afternoon writing class was over, and as is my habit, I was thinking about the topic of "names" as I walked along Jewell Avenue on the mile walk back to my place on Lighthouse Avenue in Pacific Grove. I was thinking about Erin, my oldest daughter's name as a perfect subject for the essay, and how the name meant peace in Gaelic, and the irony of Erin being anything but a peaceful child offered many possibilities for an essay.

The rest of day and evening was spent doing the mundane tasks that we all do without giving much real thought to them – the preparation of dinner, watching television, responding to some e-mails and wondering if I had any hope of winning that weekend's family football pool. Little did I realize that my life would change dramatically in just twelve short hours. I think it was John Lennon who said, "Life happens to you when you are busy making other plans."

The next morning, I awoke at 5:20 am and reached for the travel clock on my bedside table to push the light button so I could see the time. In a subtle way my left hand trembled, I fumbled with the clock, it fell to the floor, and even though I was not fully awake I sensed something was not right. My left hand did not feel right, it was tight, and my hand and fingers tingled in a way that felt they were disconnected from me. As my head cleared, I reached for a book on my bed; once again I fumbled and dropped the book. I was not sure what had happened, but somehow during the night I had lost coordination and strength in my left hand and arm. I got up and went into the bathroom, and the strange, out of body feeling persisted. I rinsed out my mouth and tried to brush my teeth. I fumbled at a task that I had been doing naturally and without much thought or concentration for all of my life. Something was definitely wrong. I even bumped the wall going into the bathroom with my left side, as if I were drunk and out of control.

It was like I was having an out of body experience where the left side of my body seemed to be disconnected or short-circuited from the command center of my brain.

What followed in rapid succession was a series of phone calls I barely remember making – to my brother in San Francisco; call to the advice nurse at the hospital; the advice nurse, "call 911"; the 911 operator, "Sir, sit down and get comfortable, someone will be coming soon." In the series of phone calls there came at some point the heart-stopping, brain-freezing, terrifying word - Stroke. Few words or phrases in the English language carry the power or can conjure up the immediate images and fear as the word Stroke.

Within two minutes of my 911 call, the ambulance and fire truck arrived at the front curb with red lights flashing and sirens wailing. Before I could process what was happening, I was being wheeled out on a gurney for a quick trip to the hospital. As we rode to the hospital, I was able to call my daughter Erin and talk to her briefly before my cell phone ran out of its charge. I briefly told her what had happened, and she started to weep before I could complete the call. At that moment, I realized how precious life was to me, and above all, I prayed to live long enough to see my two grandchildren I had at that time grow up and achieve their dreams and milestones. I wanted to be "Poppa" a lot longer.

As we made our way to the hospital, I wondered why the ambulance was taking the scenic route, and the fact there were no red lights and sirens on this trip was somehow calming to me as I watched the passing scene out the rear window, where I viewed where we had been and not where we were going. There was some symbolism and meaning there, but it somehow eluded me.

After arriving in the emergency section at Community Hospital, the rest of the day became a jumble of cardiology, radiology, neurology, I-Vs, EKGs, CT scan, MRI, vital signs, blood tests, urine tests, arteries, veins, capillaries, gurneys, punctuated by thoughts of why the hospital gown never seemed to fully close in the rear, and why did I feel like a first grader as I struggled to sign my name on various hospital forms amid concern that my life would never be the same again as I lay in a hospital bed staring at various posters and announcements. There was even a bit of comic relief when the ambulance crew, transporting me to another hospital, mistakenly delivered me to the wrong hospital in San Jose.

In the end, there was the soothing reassurance and comfort of the powerful words "minor or mini-stroke," "prognosis of a full recovery in time," discharge from the hospital, no restrictions; relief ---

Now, what about the meaning of the name Erin…

"Something Has Happened"

"Something has happened." Those simple words, announced at the Child Support Conference opening session in September 2001, have remained imprinted on my memory, my heart and my soul ever since they were spoken, like some memories in our lifetime that are never forgotten: hearing that President Kennedy had been assassinated in 1963; or recalling where I was and how I felt when I experienced a particularly strong earthquake in 1957 in San Francisco; or recalling that rainy, Friday night in the fall of the early 1960s when I heard that a former elementary school classmate and friend had been killed in an automobile accident. The emotions, feelings, and thoughts always seem to remain close to the surface and are easily recalled, maybe too easily.

I was at the Hyatt Crystal City Hotel in Arlington, Virginia, across the Potomac River from Washington DC and close to the nearby National Airport. The welcoming and introductory speeches had been concluded by the federal government secretary of this or undersecretary of that and the six hundred or so attendees from throughout the United States were beginning to restlessly gather up our belongings and head to various meeting rooms for our individual sessions. I was to present a workshop on California's innovative hospital-based paternity establishment program in the very first round of workshops during the first day of the three-day conference.

I was distracted and not fully paying attention when the Health and Welfare Undersecretary returned to the microphone and somberly announced, "Can you all remain seated, I have an announcement to make: **"Something has happened."** These simple words, **"Something has happened"** somehow struck me as unusual or out of place in a setting of formal speeches by government bureaucrats. He then proceeded to calmly and slowly explain that "Two planes have crashed into the Twin Towers in New York City, and although we are not sure at this time, these plane crashes may have been deliberate."

Gasps, murmurs and muted cries erupted throughout the room in reaction to the announcement. The information available at the time of his announcement was sketchy and brief, but somehow those in the audience sensed or understand that **"something major had happened."** At the time of the announcement in that basement ballroom, none of us knew that our lives would never be the same, nor did we know that almost at the moment the announcement was being made, a third plane had crashed into the Pentagon only a few miles away from our hotel.

At that point, each one of us in attendance was left with our own thoughts about how the events in New York City would impact us in Washington DC. Our first instinct was to find a television set so we could get an update on what was happening. For me, I thought of my nephew Dennis from Wichita, Kansas, whom I was scheduled to meet for dinner later in the week, and how we had both thought of our good fortune at being in the East that week. For he was at that moment in New York City attending a business meeting, and I had no idea where he was meeting. A sinking, hollow feeling of fear for his safety took hold of me. Hours later, I was relieved to connect my first phone call in which I heard from my brother-in-law in Wichita that my nephew was safe in New York City.

Amazingly, after the announcement that **"something has happened,"** the first round of scheduled workshop sessions went on, although some of us tried to figure out whether or not to cancel our sessions. I presented my session in a daze, as five people just like me who did not know what to do with themselves after hearing the announcement. Later in the morning it was announced that the conference was canceled, and participants were left to figure out how they would get home. All Washington DC airports were closed indefinitely and all major rental car companies were putting their fleet of cars out of service.

Some lifelong, indelible images were burned into my memory that week I was stranded in the Washington DC area at the Hyatt Hotel. The first was watching the television coverage of the Pentagon crash from my seventh-floor room and seeing the view out the window behind the television – there was the actual smoke from the Pentagon billowing just over the hill from the hotel. Yes, **Something had happened**.

TIS AN ILL WIND

PART I

"Tis an ill wind that blows nobody any good." This proverb from the 1500s is one that had always fascinated me because I could not think of any disaster, catastrophe or tragedy that did not benefit someone.

The wind in 1986 came into our neighborhood in the suburbs of Sacramento in the form of flooding due to the oversaturated ground from weeks of rain, releases of water from the Folsom Dam, and a barely noticeable creek aptly named Cripple Creek. In one evening, the waters rose to a level that flooded half of the homes on our cul-de-sac before the flood waters receded the following morning. The flood caused hundreds of thousands of dollars in property damage while disrupting the lives of hundreds of families in our middle-class Citrus Heights neighborhood. But something good came out of the flood waters in the form of neighbors helping neighbors to whom they had barely spoken prior to the flooding: bonds and friendships developed in a few days following the flooding that would last for years. **Tis an ill wind that blows nobody any good.**

A most personal experience with the proverb came into my life in the mid-1990s in the form of a whirlwind of an Irishman named Tom.

My assignment in the child support program in the mid-1990s was to be statewide analyst responsible for the area of paternity or legal fatherhood establishment. In the child support program and area of family law, married men were legally presumed to be the biological father of the child born to their wife, while children born to unmarried women had no presumed father and paternity had to be established by the courts. From the standpoint of my job responsibilities, the area of paternity was fairly simple because most paternity issues and disputes were driven by case law and legal precedents, which were under the control of the courts and lawyers. Also, around the time I started working in the child support program, the science of DNA testing to determine paternity was passing the legal hurdles for it to be accepted as the legally approved way of establishing paternity. So, my job at that time primarily was in the area of directing the counties on procedures and regulations that they were required to follow to establish paternity.

The landscape of paternity establishment in the early 1990s was about to make a radical change and I would be on the front lines, shifting from the courtroom to birthing units in hospitals and to vital statistics agencies. Unmarried women and the fathers of their children would be given the opportunity to voluntarily establish the child's paternity in the hospital without the time and expense of going to court. The State of Washington had come up with a program to voluntarily establish paternity in the hospitals at the time of a child's birth by the completion and signing of a form by both parents under the penalty of perjury. In California, there was bipartisan support for this idea, so legislation was passed to establish a pilot study in three California counties to test the concept for a year before enacting the requirement in California.

I was offered what turned out to be the job opportunity of a lifetime by the Director of Child Support Program in California to run this pilot study. I declined the offer thinking that there would be excessive travel involved and I had been burned out on travel in a previous job with the Department of Employment. So, our department needed to hire a person to coordinate this pilot study, a person I would be required to work closely with for about six months so the person would be ready to coordinate the pilot program.

We hired a man named Tom who seemed to have perfect credentials needed for the position. Tom was a man in his mid-forties who had been born and raised in Ireland before coming to America in his early twenties. Tom had worked in a hospital medical records department and also had completed a few years of law school.

I looked forward to working with Tom, as I had become interested in my Irish ancestry and thought I could learn much about Ireland from him. But from the first day working with Tom, I realized it would be a challenge to work with him. For Tom very quickly demonstrated that he was a know-it-all, an arrogant man with an attitude with a capital "A". For some reason, he wanted to provoke and incite those around him. The challenge for me was that I had to mentor, train and work very closely with a man who felt that he already knew it all. I had never had conflicts with my colleagues and always considered myself a team player in the office environment. I worked very hard to get along with Tom and overlook his attitude and arrogance. After working with this man for just a few days, I dreaded coming to work and came to the conclusion that I could not work with him on such a close basis. Because we worked in an annex room, apart from others in our unit, I was virtually sequestered with Tom for eight hours a day. I started to wonder if it was me or Tom who was the problem.

The rest of my six-person unit and our supervisor came to know "my Tom" on the Friday of his first week on the job when we went out to lunch at a local café to celebrate my birthday. Tom proceeded to show his lack of judgment when he ordered the "beer sampler" and downed the six small beers in quick succession. He became a bit tipsy and took front and center stage when he informed us about his marital separation. I recall thinking that this was his very first social outing with his new work colleagues and he was entertaining us with personal details of his marital separation? Tom told us he should have known his marriage was on shaky grounds when his wife objected to one of his home routines. He said he would watch sports on TV and, like any red-blooded fan, he accompanied his viewing with beer consumption. He said he would roll each of his empty beer bottles down the stairs and tell his wife to put them in the garbage. Tom jokingly said that when she started to object, he knew his marriage might be in trouble. He thought this story was funny and chuckled as he concluded it. We sat in stunned silence at the end of this tale told by a man we hardly knew. What in the world was this guy thinking?

At the end of the day, Linda, my supervisor, called me into to her office; I had expected her to ask me about the episode with Tom at the restaurant. But she just asked me how my first week with Tom had gone. I decided to take the middle or high road, and rather than say I was having serious problems with Tom and could not stand working with him, I told her we were adjusting to each other and things were progressing. In other words, I said nothing because I knew that in the end, it would ultimately be Linda's decision whether Tom would pass probation and make it in our office. Linda dropped a bit of a hint as to her own misgivings about Tom when she said she had discussed and reviewed with him the standards she expected him to meet in our office.

Tom's second week in our office was more of the same with the attitude, the arrogance, and the know-it-all behavior. I wondered if he had some personal issues or problems and his bravado front was his way of hiding or compensating for some insecurity. Whatever the reason for his behavior, Tom was becoming my problem, as I found it an intolerable working relationship and our work was not getting done. I dreaded that I would have to spend a week with this man on an upcoming fact-finding trip to Washington State we were scheduled to take in a few weeks. Something had to give, and soon.

And something did give, in a most shocking way imaginable within the week. It all started with a phone call Tom received later that week.

PART II

After receiving the phone call, Tom came out of his cubicle and the man I saw had been stripped of all his bravado and arrogance. He looked like the cliché – the man who had seen a ghost or had lost his best friend. He stumbled and stuttered a bit when he told me he needed some time off and was going to tell our supervisor that he needed to go home for the rest of the day. I actually found myself feeling sorry for him briefly – very briefly. He obviously had received some bad or troubling news in that phone call. But as he left the office, I recall that he had previously looked down his nose at me when he told me that he was an "academic" and not merely some state bureaucrat and, by inference, had told me that I was merely a state bureaucrat. Also, he had told me about his brother who had a loving family, lived in the suburbs and loved to watch football and baseball on the weekends. He called his brother's existence "banal." Well, being that he had pretty much described my existence, which was much like his brother's, "banal bureaucrat" had stuck in my mind.

Following Tom's departure for the day, my supervisor Linda called me in to her office and told me that Tom had received some troubling news and was taking the rest of the day off to deal with it. Linda told me that she was giving me this personal information only because Tom and I were work partners and the information might have an impact on our work. She added that I should not discuss this with others in the office. Linda told me that the call Tom had received was from a nineteen-year-old man who claimed that he was Tom's son from a college relationship and the son wanted to meet with Tom. The man said his mother had only just revealed Tom's identity and now that he was an adult it would be up to him if he wanted to try to contact Tom. Tom claimed he was totally ignorant of the fact that he had fathered a son. In fact, he had told us in no uncertain terms that he neither had nor wanted children. The information that he might be a father to a nineteen-year-old had stunned Tom, and he needed some time off to process the information. The irony of the situation was not lost on either Linda or me. Here was Tom, who had just started a job in the field of paternity establishment, and he was being called up to deal with his very own potential paternity.

When Tom returned to work the following day, he was not reticent about discussing the situation, and he had regained some of his bluster and confidence. He told us the basic facts provided by the caller – I don't think he ever referred to him as his son – were accurate about a woman he had a brief fling with in college and who had quickly disappeared from Tom's life. The young man wanted to meet with Tom. Tom's questions and dilemma were much the same as many who had been faced with a question of paternity. Was he, in fact, the biological father of this man who he did not know? What exactly did the man want by contacting him at this time in his life? What were his legal and personal responsibilities to this man? As these and many other questions swirled around in Tom's mind, his immediate concern was, would he meet with the man? And when?

By the end of the week, Tom had decided he would meet with the man during the coming weekend, but he did not share any of the details of the meeting with his coworkers. I think a part of Tom liked the attention he received in the office as the week's number one topic of office gossip. We were all interested in how Tom's situation would be handled and what would happen when Tom met with "his son." For me, I sensed the situation had humbled Tom and actually improved our working relationship. But in reality, the situation had created a distraction that had virtually halted any work Tom was doing. In the future, we would have to make up for lost time.

On the following Monday, Tom failed to show up for work and did not call in to report the reason for his absence. What started out in our office with some jokes about Tom's confrontation with his alleged son, turned into genuine concern as the time passed with no word from Tom. We finally received a call from his estranged wife, who said Tom had a serious accident over the weekend and he was in the intensive care unit at a local hospital with a severe head injury.

Tom had taken a serious fall down the long, steep outside stairs at a local restaurant-bar. There were no witnesses to the fall, nor did Tom have any recollection of what had happened. His wife later said that despite his exterior bravado, Tom was very upset and shaken by the revelation of his alleged paternity claimed by the nineteen-year-old man. She confirmed that Tom had postponed the meeting with the young man and she inferred that Tom may have been drinking prior to his fall.

Tom spent weeks in Intensive Care and he did not recall much from the recent past, which included his time in the paternity program and the contact he had with the young man claiming to be his son. Some of us visited Tom in the hospital; he seemed confused and befuddled by his situation and he did not recognize us. His wife had said quite seriously that he was a lot nicer now than he was before his fall.

Over time, we learned that Tom had been transferred to a rehabilitation facility in the San Francisco Bay Area and he was facing a long period of rehabilitation. It was unlikely that he would be returning to work. We were left to wonder what role the contact from "his son" had played in the circumstances that led to Tom's accident. Also, we wondered if he would sufficiently recover to resolve the situation with the "son" and if he would ever be able to return to work.

With Tom's future uncertain, I was assigned to head up the three-county paternity pilot study, and I had very short time to pull together all the elements required by the legislation. And later, I was part of the team that implemented the program that became mandatory at the more than three hundred birthing hospitals in California. It turned out to be the most demanding but also the most rewarding job in my life. It was a program that I believed in and one that would have a positive impact on the lives of hundreds of thousands of fathers and their children – a state program that actually worked the way it was intended to in the legislation and would make a difference in lives of many parents and their children. It was a great experience for me to work with county paternity experts, vital statistics agencies and dedicated birth clerks and nurses at hospitals throughout California. These were the people who made this program the great success it became. I felt proud to have been a part of it. And although I never wished anything bad to happen to Tom, I sincerely believed that his presence in the program would have been disastrous, because his arrogance and condescension would not have worked in a program requiring tact and diplomacy.

"Tis an ill wind that blows nobody any good." The ill wind for Tom had blown much good my way.

Epilogue

More than a year later, after Tom's accident, our office received a scrawled, handwritten, barely decipherable note from Tom, requesting reinstatement. The review of his situation and his medical condition by doctors, lawyers and administrators determined that because he had never completed probation with our program, the decision with regard to his reinstatement rested with his prior department. Their review of his case determined that he had falsified his application and resume with our department, and the person he identified as his last manager was actually a friend who lied when he was interviewed about Tom's job qualifications. We never heard if Tom ever established a relationship with the man who had claimed to have been his son.

My Friend Donald - Making A Difference

I moved to Pacific Grove, California, on the Monterey Peninsula in 2006 following my retirement from the State of California in Sacramento. For me, it was something of a daring move, as I did not know anyone in the community. At first, it was a bit hard for me to make friends in the small community until I joined to Forty Plus Senior Group at St. Angela Merici Church. I noticed this man about my age sometimes attending church. Although he was balding, I noticed he had long hair in a ponytail coming out the back of his ball cap. My mind said – a hippie from the 1960s. I often saw this man walking all over the Monterey Peninsula.

One day I saw him in the local coffee shop and he was fiddling with his smartphone. I had wanted to learn more about smartphones and I thought talking to a man about my age would be a less intimidating way to find out more about the phones. The man's name was Donald Dwight, and I learned we had much in common. He was a retired government accountant from the Department of Defense, having worked at Fort Ord and the Presidio of Monterey. He was separated from his wife of many years and he had two young adult children although they were not married, and he did not have any grandchildren. Donald was like myself, a graduate of a California State College (he had graduated from Fresno State while I was a graduate of San Francisco State College). Over time we became friends, regularly having coffee and lunch together.

My friend Donald told me that he had cancer, a unique form of cancer that caused clusters of tumors to grow internally. He informed me that the condition had been treated with increasing levels of medication that kept the tumors from growing and spreading. But after a few years of having the condition controlled by the medication, in mid-2014 the dosage of his medication had reached its limit. He learned he was a candidate for inclusion in a new drug trial through research being conducted at Stanford University Medical Center. Because of pain medication Donald was taking, he was not able to drive himself to Stanford for his examinations and laboratory tests that went with the drug research. I was happy to help him in a small way by driving him up to Stanford Medical Center a few times.

Donald was in his initial stage of the trial, having taken the new medication for a few weeks when he was scheduled for blood tests and his first major examination by the clinical research team at Stanford. When I picked him up that morning I was a bit alarmed to see his appearance. His skin had a yellowish tinge and he was a bit more drawn in appearance than usual. I tried not to show my alarm and just inquired as to how he was feeling. He said he was feeling fine and seemed to be unaware of his drastic change in appearance.

The trip to Stanford was my first visit to the Stanford Cancer Center. In keeping with the name and reputation associated with Stanford, there was a feeling of excellence about the place, from the valet parking that greeted us at the entrance to the quiet piano player in the lobby, to the artwork, to the fountains and gardens; the facility had an atmosphere of being very special. Everything about the facility quietly spoke a message of quality, excellence, and innovation of what is a renowned facility that is recognized as one of the leaders in the field of cancer treatment and research.

For Donald, it was hours of testing and examinations prior to meeting with his clinical team of four doctors, a clinical researcher and a support staff of academic and medical professionals. For me, it was a time to explore the facility and wait. For those waiting there was a nice café, a small cafeteria and quiet area for reading or connecting to the Internet.

Sitting in the waiting area, I was deeply into a book when Donald quietly approached me. He said, "Jim, there are some people here who would like to talk to you."

I looked up, and standing in front of me was Donald's clinical team of four young women in white doctor's coats. The lead doctor proceeded to explain to me that Donald's tests had revealed an abnormality in his liver function and they needed me to be clear about what needed to be done for Donald. Donald needed to immediately return to the Monterey Peninsula and see his personal physician (an appointment had already been set by the Stanford team with Donald's physician in Monterey). The doctor explained to me in clear and concise language what the problem was and how important my role was to be in transporting him back to Monterey. Few times in my life can I recall being treated with such respect and dignity by professionals like this. Although they did not come out and say it, their message was loud and clear: You are important in Donald's care; today what you are doing is going to make a difference.

  Donald and I returned to Monterey and we visited with his personal physician, who made the decision that Donald needed to be admitted to Community Hospital. Donald was treated for a few days in the hospital and was discharged when his liver functioning returned to normal.

  Thinking back on that day, I came to the conclusion that every person at that cancer center was making a difference, from the valets who helped us with our car, to the volunteer musician who played the piano in the lobby, to the friends and family who provided the support and companionship, to the patients, to doctors, nurses, support staff, technicians and volunteers. Each one played a vital role in making a difference in the lives of those patients. And I realized that for each one of us there are opportunities to make a difference almost every day – all we have to do is to be aware of those opportunities and seize them when they present themselves to us.

Donald D Dwight
March 2, 1940 - October 12, 2014

LIFE AND DEATH - HOPE AND DESPAIR

The two news reports appearing within days of each other are jarring, jolting and unsettling. In Bellflower, California, a woman gives birth to eight children with over forty medical professionals assisting in the birth and care of the mother and children. Mother and children are doing well. A few days later, it is reported that a man who has had been fired from his job has murdered his five children and his wife before killing himself. All of the children were under the age of seven. The murder-suicide occurred in Wilmington, California, just a few miles from where the woman had given birth to the eight children. The woman had given birth to the children at a Kaiser Hospital and the deceased man and his wife had both been fired from another Southern California Kaiser Hospital. Although the events reported in the two stories had occurred within miles of each other, the people involved had lived lives worlds apart.

Life and Death; Hope and Despair.

We have all experienced to varying degrees the extremes that life has to offer – Life and death; hope and despair.

The baby cries and life begins; the telephone rings in the middle of the night, what news does it bring; the stomach churns, the palms perspire, the test results are in – benign or malignant; a scream is heard – is it of joy or of pain; the touchdown is scored and the celebration begins; the batter has whiffed in the bottom of the ninth with the base loaded; a tear slowly runs down the child's cheek; **It's a BOY**!; **It's CANCER!**; the notice of promotion comes in; the layoff notice goes out; the tires screech, the glass shatters, we hold our breath, we say a silent prayer; you **got an A! Congratulations! – You got an F – Commiseration;** the sun has broken through the clouds; the window has been opened, the fresh air comes in; the door has slammed shut as your child stomps out; I am so happy for you; sorry to hear about that.

Eight babies born in Bellflower; five babies killed in Wilmington.

THE MYSTERY AND JOY OF LIFE

(To my grandchildren) "I may not be the most important person
in your life, I just hope when you hear my name
you will smile and think, 'that's my Poppa'."
Jim Mullany

PART I

"Do you believe that God gives us only the challenges in life that we are capable of handling?" As soon as the question was out of my mouth, I thought of how inappropriate and awkward it was to be posing this question to my son-in-law Leo. I was asking him about one of life's real mysteries. We were in the Women's and Children's section of the Kaiser Hospital in Roseville, California, where my daughter Erin had been admitted a few days earlier in mid-June, 2011, having commenced labor three months premature to her early in October due date. Erin and Leo had gone to the hospital for a routine pregnancy medical examination on June 14th when she suddenly went into labor. She was admitted to the hospital and labor had been stopped, at least temporarily. In terms of her pregnancy, Erin was in her twenty-third week and although she was thirty-eight years old, it was way too early for Erin to deliver her first child. A "normal pregnancy" lasts forty weeks or nine months, so this was way, way too early.

I had arrived from Pacific Grove a few days after Erin was admitted to the hospital in order to lend any moral or personal support I could, as Erin would be hospitalized indefinitely while she was administered a drug to delay her labor as long as possible. In addition, she would try to consume as many calories as possible to increase the size and strength of the baby. It was a scary, nervous and traumatic time for all of the family, but most especially for Erin and Leo.

Leo had explained to me the hospital processes they had endured when it appeared that Erin was going to deliver prematurely earlier in the week. He said everything had been routine and uneventful until that afternoon when their world was turned upside down. He said one moment the most important decision they had to make was what they were going to have for dinner that evening. Then in what seemed like an instant, they were being counseled and asked to make life and death decisions about what life-saving efforts and procedures the hospital should employ to save the child should he be born right then. He said it was one of the most emotional and scary moments of their lives. Decisions they had not even considered or discussed would be required of them to make virtually in an instant.

While Erin was in premature labor, she and Leo were presented with an array of stark facts in making decisions relative to their baby, if he was to be born at the twenty-third week of her pregnancy; the chances were eight in ten that the baby would die and life support would only delay the inevitable. If the baby was to be born, extraordinary measures would need to be employed, and all of the medical knowledge and resources would need to be marshaled for the baby to survive. Cold statistics told them what might happen to the baby should he survive and the various developmental problems a surviving child born at twenty-three weeks potentially might face. Leo said the way it had been presented to them in the instance of a birth before twenty-six weeks, the life-saving decisions were the province of the parents, as most babies born prior to twenty-six weeks were not likely to survive without life support, while those babies who are born at twenty-six weeks and beyond had a survival rate of 90%.

What parents are able to make such life and deaths decisions when they have a reasonable amount of time to consider the options, conduct research and discuss the consequences of their decision, much less those who face such decisions at a time of the gravest medical and personal crisis of their lives? Leo explained it was a nightmare of epic portions when in a fragile emotional state. They were faced with legal documents listing catastrophic medical consequences and told they must make these decisions in what seemed like an instant.

Part II

It was in this context that I had asked Leo that question about the challenges we are presented and what we are capable of handling. Upon reflection, it seemed so wrong and inappropriate for me to pose the question under those circumstances. But Leo did not hesitate in answering. "Jim, I believe we are given much more than we can handle as a way for us to grow and test us with regard to what challenges we are capable of handling." He added although it was a very difficult time for him and Erin, he felt he was ready to handle whatever might happen, and that we needed to provide Erin with all the love and support we could.

For Leo, who was in his mid-forties, this was not the first life and death crisis he had dealt with. He had already faced the ultimate crisis that is any parent's worst nightmare and far beyond any event or challenge most of us would ever face in our lives. The situation Leo and his family had dealt with was so tragic that it was newsworthy in Sacramento. Leo's eight-year-old daughter had died in a swimming pool accident.

The grief, anger, guilt, and depression from this event in 2004 had been present with Leo since his daughter's death, and it was something that he had endured when I had posed that question to him in June of 2011, while he provided support, comfort, and strength to my daughter in Kaiser Hospital. Our children should not die before us. If one of them does, it amounts to one of life's great tragedies. How does one handle it or endure it? Challenges – if anyone knew about challenges, Leo knew about life's challenges. And here, Leo was once again facing a new life and death challenge. What was going to happen, how were we all going to make it through this crisis?

PART III

The family was thrilled in 2011 when we learned that my oldest daughter Erin was pregnant in her late thirties with her first child – a boy. She married Leo in the summer of 2009 in a beautiful beach wedding in Kauai, Hawaii. The first two years of their marriage had been idyllic, with them competing in Triathlons while also traveling a bit. It was exciting and thrilling when we learned that they would be having a baby boy in October 2011. I loved being a grandparent to Avery and Cameron, the children born to my daughter Adrienne and her husband. I had never envisioned the happiness and just plain fun grandchildren could bring into your life. In our families with more females than males, my two sons-in-law and I were delighted to have another male to help equalize things out.

On June 14, everything changed in our family – and in our world. On that day I received a phone call from Erin's mother. Bonnie and I knew immediately that something was wrong. Bonnie did not call me to chit chat; most calls between us involved our daughters or our grandchildren. Although it was granddaughter Avery's fourth birthday, our plans were to celebrate it on the coming Saturday in San Jose with Avery's dance performance and a family birthday party.

Bonnie told me that Erin had gone to her regularly scheduled doctor's appointment at the Kaiser Hospital in Roseville, California and she had suddenly gone into labor. The news took my breath away because I knew without any calculation that this was way too early for Erin to be delivering the baby, which not due until early October. It was a very serious situation. Bonnie reassured me that the good thing about the situation was she was right there at the hospital when the labor started and she was immediately admitted to the hospital. The goal of her treatment was to stop the labor for as long as possible and for her to remain in the hospital indefinitely on bed rest and to receive treatment to delay her labor as long as possible.

Erin was to remain calm and not to get excited; she was to consume as many calories as possible so the baby within her would grow and develop as much as possible before the birth. Her delivery could be in a day, a week, a month or three months, but the prognosis was that she would remain in the hospital until she delivered the baby. The pressure and stress on Erin were intense because she was in a very fragile state and it was not known what or why she had gone into premature labor. Her health was excellent, and she had none of the obvious risk factors that might cause an expectant woman to suddenly go into labor. Her diet and nutrition were excellent, she had exercised regularly, and she was very knowledgeable on how to care for herself. Her life was suddenly measured by the fraction of weeks that were recorded on the whiteboard in her hospital room. It had started at twenty-three weeks, and each day she got through would be an additional one-seventh added to her countdown chart on that whiteboard.

Erin's situation was a perfect example of the old saying, life happens while you are making other plans. In our family's case, plans were being made for a normal pregnancy and delivery, with baby showers, baby furniture, baby clothes and a baby room being prepared with plenty of time available for the baby to arrive, when all of a sudden, all of those plans are out the window and the reality is a life or death struggle had to be waged in a quiet, modern hospital room in the Sacramento Valley. Life was now happening minute to minute and hour to hour, and there were no other plans to be made.

PART IV

I went up to the Sacramento area to visit Erin while she was hospitalized at the Roseville Kaiser Hospital in mid-June and I was struck by the many contrasts present. First, there was the searing summer heat outside the hospital in the Sacramento Valley in June, compared to the coolness of the-state-of-the-art hospital room at the Women's and Children's Center at the Kaiser Hospital. Erin was a very active young woman involved in competing in triathlons, she loved to tend to her garden, and she worked full time for Campbell Soup in the Purchasing Department, yet here she was in a hospital bed with the charge of having to remain inactive for what could be days, weeks or months. Not only did she have to remain calm and inactive, she had to be in that state while trying to consume as many calories as possible in order to ensure the growth and nutrients of the baby. It was not an easy situation she had to endure, and so her family and friends tried to offer her as much support, encouragement and understanding and subdued companionship as was possible under the circumstances.

The hospital environment where Erin was situated was a bit surreal, as for the most part the Women's and Children's Center was a modern state-of-the-art birthing center where women in labor came to give birth, stay for a day or two to recover and then be discharged. Unlike the rest of the hospital, where sick or injured people came to be treated, this was a place for the most part that was of joy and celebration. Friends and family members could be seen arriving with flowers, candy, balloons and stuffed animals to celebrate with the new mothers the arrival of a new infant; it was generally a happy, joyous event celebrated in a happy, joyous environment. But the center did have a few long-term "patients," including women like Erin who were seeking to delay labor, and the infants down in the basement, a neonatal and pediatric intensive care unit. The tone and environment of the Women's and Children's Center were one of short transition and a joyous celebratory discharge.

On my second trip from Pacific Grove to up to Sacramento to spend time Erin in early July she was relatively stable, so I felt she was going to be able to stall labor for weeks or months, and I returned to Pacific Grove on July 3rd.

On July 4th, I received a telephone message from Erin informing me she was now in a different room at the hospital. When I called her later that afternoon, she asked me if I was not going to ask her why she was had been transferred to another room? She did not wait for my question but just said with joy in her voice, "**Because I had a baby this afternoon!**" A boy named Ian Scarborough had entered the world weighing two pounds and fraction less than six ounces, arriving in Erin's twenty-sixth week of pregnancy. Ian was what is called a micro-preemie and was among only one percent of the babies born in the United States during the mother's twenty-sixth week of pregnancy. Erin informed me that Ian had been immediately placed in the neonatal intensive care unit of the hospital and he would be receiving the best possible care. Hanging up the phone, I realized that this was only the beginning of the story.

PART V

A few days later, Erin called me to inform me that they had given Ian the middle name of James in honor of his "Poppa" – me. I was greatly honored and touched by this gesture, and at that point, I silently vowed to myself from that day forward I would always refer to and call him "Ian James," not just Ian. For the connection that had been forged with the name James would forever connect Ian James to my family – my father was named James, and my grandfather on my mother's side was also named James. And although neither of those relatives of Ian James were around to know him and love him as I would, they would forever be linked to that micro preemie baby who would be treated in the NICU at Kaiser Hospital in Roseville for the next three months. My eyes welled up as I wished that both my father and grandfather were still around to share the honor of our naming connection to little Ian James Scarborough. I sobbed in my solitude and I said a silent prayer for little Ian James and the fragile beginning of his life.

Before my first visit to see Ian James in the NICU (the Neonatal Intensive Care Unit) my son-in-law Leo briefed me about the unit and the policy and procedures that had to be strictly followed. As a rule, only two people at a time were allowed to visit a baby in the unit, and generally one of those people had to be a parent of the child. The second visitor had to be approved by the parents, and for the most part, these approved visitors were adult relatives of the parents such as grandparents, siblings and so on. An exception might be made when both parents were visiting and a third person would be permitted in the unit, depending upon the condition of the baby. All of these procedures had been developed over the years to protect the health and well-being of the fragile infants housed in the NICU.

Before entering the NICU, all visitors were required to present identification, and from the identification, a personalized identification badge was created that included the photo and identification information of the visitor and indicated the visitor was allowed in the NICU. The unit was housed in the basement of the Women's and Children's Health

Center, and to get to the actual NICU you were required to pass through two locked security entrances where you buzzed in, after speaking into an intercom and being viewed by a remote camera controlled by an unseen security officer.

The NICU was divided into about ten individualized units, each housing six to eight infants who were at varying levels of intensive care. As a micro-preemie weighing just over two pounds and being born in the twenty-sixth week of my daughter's pregnancy, I suspect that for the first few weeks of his care, Ian James was housed in the unit providing the highest level of care. Upon entering the unit, the first impression one has is how quiet it is and how subdued the lighting is. There is a feeling of solemn reverence and respect for life that permeates the entire unit. It is like entering the church or a place of reverence. I have never been in an environment where I have ever felt there was such reverence, respect and care for life as I felt in the NICU. There were not the sounds and activity one normally associates with a hospital, but rather the feeling there was the utmost sensitivity and care to the fragility of the young patients being cared for in this room, those who lives were hanging in the balance. There was none of that casual feeling of life being taken for granted that one experiences in everyday life present here; nothing was taken for granted in this unit.

The first requirement was that all electronic devices were to be turned off; then there was the cleanliness issue, with all entering the NICU being required to wash their hands and arms thoroughly all the way up to the elbows, followed by the application of germicidal gel.

Leo had told me that all talk was to be done softly, not necessarily a whisper but softly and calmly, so not to disturb the fragility of the patients being treated in this unit. Due to the sensitivity of all the babies being treated, the privacy of the other patients and visitors in the unit were to be respected at all times, with no staring at others or interaction with them at any time nor any inquiries made about the other babies. Each pod or incubator in the unit that was occupied was a life and a story and a struggle for each family involved, and the sensitive and fragile nature of each must be respected.

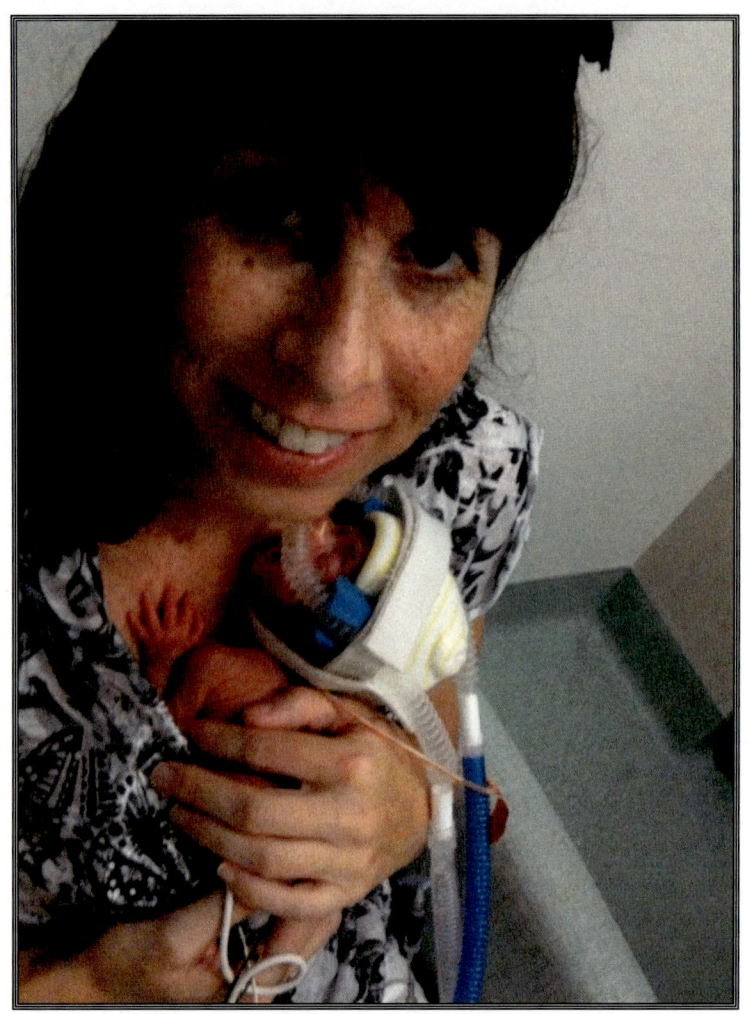
Erin with tiny Ian James in Intensive Care

I came to visit Ian James for the first time during the first week of his life in early July; the contrast between the searing heat of the Sacramento Valley summer outside, and the climate-controlled environment in the NICU was startling. Ian James, like all the other babies in the NICU, was housed in an incubator-like infant warmer bed, which was a clear plastic pod unit that had a removable top section. The unit was heated by a radiant warmer when the unit was closed or had heat circulating at a constant temperature when the top of the unit was open. Although I had mentally prepared myself to see Ian for the first time by picturing his tiny size, it was still startling to see him for the first time. He was so tiny! His weight fluctuated from his birth weight of two pounds six ounces all the way down to one pound, nine ounces. He wore a little elf-type cap to keep his head warm, and the tiniest diaper I had ever seen in my life, about the size of a book of matches. His skin had a healthy pink glow to it, and he did appear to be a regular baby except for his micro size.

It was not just the size of Ian James that had startled me, but rather all the wires, tubes and monitors that were attached to his tiny body that reminded me of how fragile the health of a baby born so early really was. There seemed to be more wires, tubes, and monitors than there was of Ian James to attach them to. Being born at twenty-six weeks and at such a small size, he was in the highest level of infant care – Level 3 – following his birth. He needed help. He was on a ventilator to help him breathe; he had a feeding tube and IV to help him get the proper amount of fluids, nutrition and medications he needed; he was attached to a cardio-respiratory monitor that kept track of his heart rate and respiratory rate; he had a temperature probe, which was a wire attached to his skin to measure and monitor his temperature; and his unit had a phototherapy light which helped to prevent and treat jaundice. These monitors, tubes, and wires were a constant in Ian James's young life – twenty-four/seven. The NICU and the electronic and technological instruments it housed were a reflection of the triumphs and advancement of modern medical science. Their purpose was to help finish and assist the work of nature or God in these most precarious infants such as Ian James. I was in awe of the NICU.

In addition to the technology and machinery that assisted Ian James, there was the NICU team, or what we came to think of as "Team Ian James." There was the neonatologist, who was the specialist in the care of preemies and infants like Ian; the team of NICU nurses who cared for Ian around the clock; and in the earliest stage he received one-to-one nursing care, twenty-four hours a day; there was the social worker who organized the needed services and coordinated the resources for the parents and family for the personal and emotional support that was needed; a respiratory therapist who delivered all the respiratory support and treatment Ian James needed throughout his stay in the NICU and ensured the maintenance of the ventilator and oxygen equipment; a nutritionist who evaluated and ensured the proper nutritional levels needed by Ian James for his proper growth; and others, including a pharmacist to manage the medications needed by Ian James and various therapists to help with movement, positioning and feeding issues.

  The environment of the Neonatal Intensive Care Unit was perfect for enabling a micro preemie such as Ian James to get all the support and treatment he needed to get through the early weeks of his life. The machines, tubes, wires, monitors and entire environment of the NICU provided all the medical support of modern science necessary to help Ian James survive those first few critical weeks of his life. But on the surface at least, the cold, sterile and artificial environment of the NICU seemed to be missing something all human beings need – the touch and contact of other humans, especially the nurturing contacts the baby had the prior six months of his development with his mother, my daughter Erin. That is where "kangaroo" or skin-to-skin care came in. Quite simply, kangaroo care was skin-to-skin contact between Ian James and his mother (and father). This "treatment" involved Ian James, wearing only a diaper, being placed on the bare chest of his mother (or father). This strategy is similar to the way a kangaroo is carried by his mother. In the case of Ian James, my daughter Erin and husband Leo tried to provide kangaroo care of Ian James for a few hours every day. The simplicity and genius of the method of care seemed to be in stark contrast to all the hours Ian James spent in the incubator-like pod of the NICU. Studies have found that as vital as all the machines, monitors and technology are to a preemie, the long periods apart from his mother were physiologically and emotionally disruptive to a baby who has been securely positioned and nurtured in his mother's womb for months. As helpful as the artificial temperature, breathing and feeding might be, the lack of physical contact with the mother might have had some really negative and counterproductive effects on Ian James.

For the three months Ian James was cared for in the NICU at Kaiser Hospital in Roseville, almost every day either Erin or Leo or oftentimes both of them, would visit and help with the care for Ian. Usually, visits would include a session of kangaroo or skin-to-skin contact with either Erin or Leo. I came to learn that this technique was a relatively new facet of preemie care that was introduced in 1978 in a hospital in Bogota, Columbia. The hospital had limited resources and a shortage of caregivers for their low weight or preemie babies, and kangaroo care was introduced to alleviate the shortages of caregivers and resources. The doctor who introduced the process simply believed that the skin-to-skin contact would help to keep the babies warm and rested during a time when incubators in the NICU were overcrowded or not available. Researchers who studied the process determined, in medical studies over the years, that the close physical contact with the parent helped to stabilize the heartbeat, temperature and the breathing of low weight or preterm infants. In addition, and of critical importance, it was found that these preemies who experienced kangaroo care had longer periods of restful sleep, they were able to more quickly gain weight, and it significantly decreased their periods of crying.

It is believed that babies in the womb sleep up to twenty hours a day during the final three months of a woman's pregnancy, which promotes the development of the vital organs prior to the birth of the child. In contrast to these long periods of sleep in the womb, when a preemie is born three months early, it is believed they only manage about two hours at a time of deep quiet sleep while in the NICU. So, sleep and the preservation of energy are the most critical factors in the care of a preemie, because those two factors are vital to the development of the critical organs of a preemie. The time of kangaroo care that Erin and Leo provided to Ian James was almost as important as all the time he spent in his incubator and pod connected to all those tubes, wires and monitors. To Erin and Leo, I think that time of skin-to-skin care was even more important for them for the natural bonding and comfort that it provided them in a time of stress and tension.

Although there would be other times of crisis during the months Ian was in the NICU, none created as much tension and anxiety as something called patent ductus arteriosus or PDA.

Part VI

Ian James Scarborough was born on July 4, 2001, more than three months premature to what would have been a full-term birth. The complications and issues in his young life were numerous, involving the formation and development of vital organs and functions. His survival was dependent upon numerous machines, tubes wires, and monitors in the intensive care unit.

One of the more serious issues little Ian faced was patent ductus arteriosus – PDA. Before a baby is born, the two major arteries in the body, the aorta and the pulmonary artery, are connected by a blood vessel called the ductus arteriosus, a vessel that is an essential part of blood circulation in an infant. In some infants, especially those born prematurely like Ian James, the ductus arteriosus, which is supposed to close, remains open, creating a condition called patent ductus arteriosus, or PDA. This opening allows oxygen-rich blood to flow to the aorta and mix with oxygen-poor blood from the pulmonary artery. This condition can put a strain on the heart and increase the blood pressure in the lung arteries. Premature babies like Ian James are quite simply more vulnerable to the effects of PDA.

For the first few weeks, it was our hopes and prayers that the ductus arteriosus would close up on it is own naturally, and surgical intervention would not be necessary. The biggest threat with PDA was potentially permanent damage to the lungs, intestines and the kidneys. As time passed into late July it looked like surgery might not be necessary, as tests indicated that the hole or opening may have been closing. But with no real warning, in late July Erin and Leo received word that the doctors had decided to perform the PDA the next day. I happened to be visiting that day when they received the word that they were to go to the hospital the following morning to receive their pre-surgery briefing and consultation. There would be no debate or discussion with regard to alternatives, as it had already been decided that the surgery was necessary, and in a micro preemie like Ian James there were no other alternatives. So, surgery it was going to be. I think the suddenness of the decision to do the surgery is what surprised us a bit, as recent information had indicated that PDA had been resolving itself.

After a long wait and some delays on the day of surgery, Erin and Leo emerged from the surgery consultation and briefing with word that Ian would be prepped for surgery and that the procedure should take about an hour and a half. The surgeon had reassured Erin and Leo that the surgical procedure needed to close a PDA was a relatively common surgery that usually had very good results, and the surgeon said that he had performed the surgery numerous times. The word "routine" was not used, as nothing about a surgery performed on a two-pound infant can be thought to be common or routine. We were apprehensive, nervous and worried about the procedure little Ian James was facing.

In this modern technological age, we were actually able to view a video of a typical PDA closure surgery on You-tube while we awaited Ian's surgery in the neonatal intensive care waiting room at Kaiser Hospital in Roseville. The small incision is done in the back and the PDA is accessed through the ribs at the rear. The surgical instruments used almost seem tiny and the vessels being repaired seem microscopic, requiring great skill on the part of the surgeon.

We settled into the waiting room for our wait. Anyone who has ever been in that situation of waiting for a critical event to be completed knows the feeling of anxiety, tension, and nervousness that makes the time almost stand still. We made small talk and we waited; we stood up and paced and we waited; we sat down and we walked and we waited: we watched people passing through the waiting room and we looked at the immovable clock and we waited, and we were left to drift into our own thoughts. We sat there waiting, having no idea what was going on behind the scenes in the operation room. Here we were trusting what was most important in our lives to someone Erin and Leo had just met – trusting Ian James's life to this surgeon and knowing we had no other choice but to trust and to wait. We waited until the one hour and a half timeframe passed; then it was two hours and then it was two and a half hours. Something did not feel or seem right – a common operation that was due to take an hour and a half was now approaching three hours.

    Finally, a man in scrubs and surgical mask entered the waiting area. He looked weary, drawn and exhausted and we waited for his pronouncement. Without preliminaries or embellishments, he introduced himself as a surgical nurse on the team who had operated on Ian and said the operation was completed and Ian was fine. He went on to explain that Ian's PDA operation was one of the most difficult the surgeon had ever performed (I thought: not common, not routine). He said the size and location of Ian's opening had made it very difficult and the surgery had "nicked an artery" and there had been substantial bleeding. "Nicked" was a word I would describe as a minor shaving cut, not something done to an artery in a two-pound baby in an operation. The nurse went on to describe that treatment and control of the bleeding were what had prolonged the operation and Ian was fine. Erin and Leo learned later at the post-op consultation that the operation was one of the most difficult PDA surgeries the surgeon had ever performed due to the size and the location of the opening. He said it was the first time in over twenty-five years of performing this surgery that he had ever nicked an artery. With great relief and gratitude, we knew Ian James was fine and was ready to face his remaining two months in the NICU; but I thought of those words 'common' and 'routine' in reference to an operation and realized there are just no such things when it is one you love.

Epilogue

    Ian James remained in the hospital NICU for three months and he was discharged when his weight reached the level it would have been had he gone to term. The entire family celebrated and were grateful that our miracle boy was home where he belonged. Because of respiration issues, Ian James needed to be administered oxygen for a few months, and until this day he still needs regular inhaler sessions. Ian James *is now six years old, and he is a lively, spirited and happy boy with a bit of the feistiness his mom had at his age and the dancing feet and "the look" of his dad as a young boy. What a guy he is.*

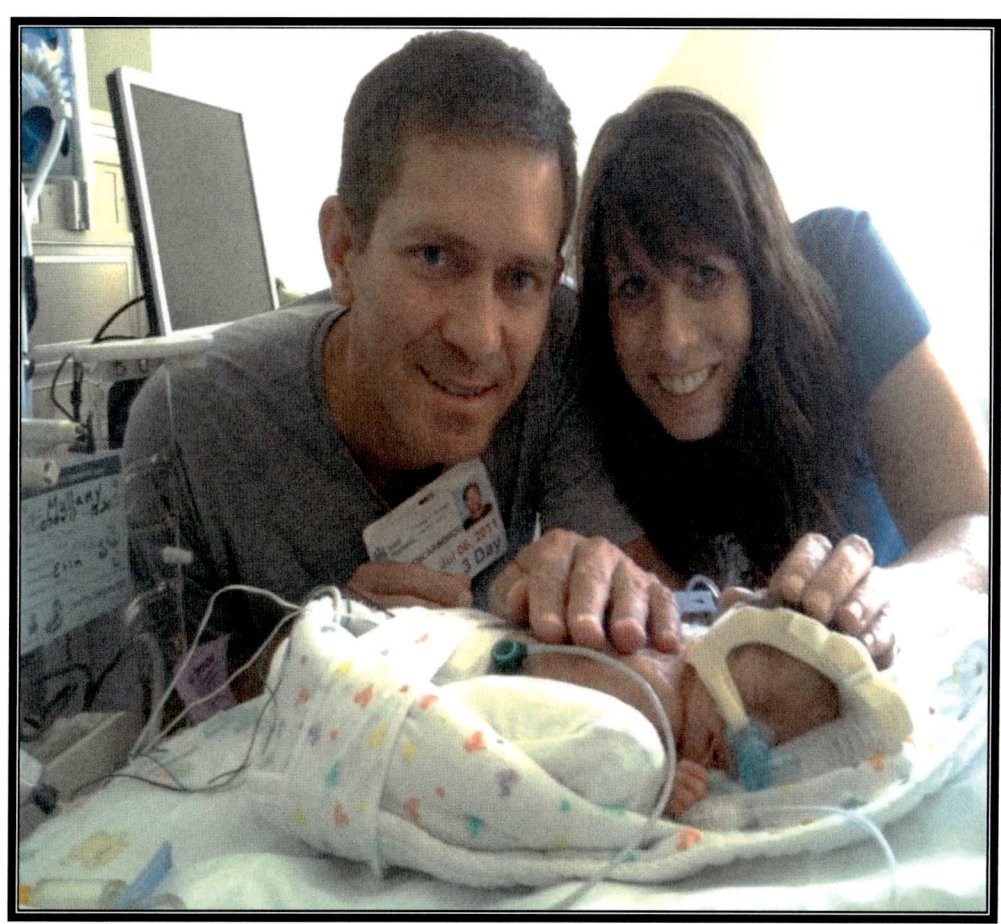

Leo, Erin and Baby Ian James – July, 2011

TRAVELS – IRELAND AND OTHER ADVENTURES

*"I have found there ain't no surer way to find out
whether you like people or hate them than to travel with them."*
Tom Sawyer Abroad – *Mark Twain*

Travel Is ...

Travel is starting a 400-mile trip from San Francisco to Los Angeles in your dad's 1948 Dodge and having it break down after motoring about one hundred yards. And after having to push-start the car, your father proclaims, "Well Boys, it's all downhill from here."

Travel is begging your father to make a bathroom stop and have him announce with a wink that a nice bathroom is just around the bend. Then you discover that the "bathroom" is a small grove of Eucalyptus trees right next to a busy highway.

Travel is having your father gloat about finding the perfect camping spot, even under the cover of darkness. One that other less skillful campers had missed. Then waking up the next morning to discover the camping spot is located almost directly beneath a sign that says "NO CAMPING PERMITTED."

Travel is agreeing to go with your father on a fishing trip to Mendocino-Fort Bragg coastal area before your wedding. And having your father announce to every gas station attendant, store clerk and fisherman he encounters, that he is "taking his son on his last bachelor's fling."

Travel is spraining your ankle on an early morning jog near Disneyland and then coming back to your room and informing your daughters that their much-anticipated day at Disneyland will have to be canceled.

Travel is limping around Disneyland for hours in pain, but constantly reassuring your daughters that, "No, it really does not hurt that much."

Travel is having your birthday reduced to just three hours due to crossing the international dateline traveling from San Francisco to Hong Kong, and having a great birthday being reunited with daughter Erin at the Hong Kong airport.

Travel is sailing out of Venice on a cruise ship as the sun is setting over St. Mark's Square and then returning days later just as the sun was rising over the Grand Canal.

Travel is side-stepping donkey dung and a donkey stampede as you climb from sea level up to town in Santorini, Greece.

Travel is my sister Maureen and I having our own personal cabbie named LeRoy to drive us all around Dunedin, New Zealand, he regaling us with stories about the cabbie named "Slippery" who our brother Mike had recommended we contact in Dunedin. Leroy advised us you never should hire a cab driver named "Slippery."

Travel is arriving in Boston and having your sister become incensed at a middle eastern cab driver who said he had never heard of Fenway Park, an icon of baseball history. Maureen muttered that no Boston cabbie could not have heard of Fenway Park.

Travel is being one of the few travelers being served a flute of champagne by a flight attendant in a darkened cabin of an Air New Zealand flight at midnight of the New Year.

Travel is having your passport stamped with the special Machu Picchu stamp.

Travel is returning home to the Monterey Peninsula, realizing there is no place in the world like this most dramatic and beautiful meeting of land and sea.

Travels With Pop

    Some of the most vivid and colorful memories of my father involve the trips we took with my older brother Mike from San Francisco to Southern California during the mid-1950s. These trips took place more than fifty years ago, but they are so clearly etched in my memory they could have taken place only yesterday. At the time of the trips, I thought the excitement and wonder of the journeys were the destinations, like Disneyland, Santa Barbara, Morro Bay and San Diego. But I now realize that the true entertainment centerpieces of those trips were not the destinations, but it was my father and his unorthodox style of traveling.

    Dad's travels usually commenced with little or no planning. Our trips to Southern California were no exception. If there was any advance planning for these trips, there was little evidence of it during our travels. He loved the sense of adventure and spontaneity that came when you arrived at a destination without reservations, maps or guidebooks. In his mind, reservations and pre-trip itineraries were for the inferior or less adventuresome travelers, not for us. This also included our automobiles in which we traveled; the cars seldom seemed to be road-worthy and were unreliable beyond short trips within San Francisco.

    Our 1956 trip down to Southern California started out in our old 1948 Dodge. It began with our inevitable loop around our block on 19th Avenue north, then around to 18th Avenue, and south back on to 19th Avenue heading south at Vicente Street. On this trip, the old car stalled out at that first signal at 19th Avenue and Vicente Street, just yards from the front of our house. Mike and I were enlisted to push-start the car, and as we hopped back into the rolling auto, Dad reassured us with that twinkle in his eye, "Boys it's all downhill from here – 500 miles downhill." I was mortified by the fact that he didn't hesitate a second to continue the trip in a car that had failed to negotiate the first very first block of the journey. It did not seem to be a good omen to me.

Years later we learned that Dad did not even have a valid driver's license back then, or for about thirty years after that trip. No worry, as my dad turned the driving over to my fifteen-year-old brother for most of the trip and Mike had neither a valid driver's license nor a permit.

Late one evening we arrived at Refugio State Beach campground, near Santa Barbara. Setting up our tent in almost total darkness, my father gloated a bit about finding such a choice camping that other campers had missed. At around 2:00 am, we were awakened by the distant sound of a freight train that became ominously louder by the second as it approached us. My brother Mike whispered to me, "Pop didn't set up our tent on railroad tracks, did he?" Just then, a heart-pounding, teeth-rattling, roaring locomotive passed just about twenty feet overhead. We had set up our tent directly beneath a low railroad bridge.

The next morning, my father's only comment was, "Boys, you'll remember that train last night long after you have forgotten about the rides in Disneyland." You know, he was right!

Later on, that same trip, we were searching for a campground in La Costa in San Diego County. Once again, it was dark as we searched for the La Costa campground and my father beamed when he saw the sign – La Costa Campground ahead. My father was delighted that we had such a nice wide-open area to set up our tent, with no other campers nearby. The next morning, we awoke early to the sound of nearby traffic. We had set up our tent right next to the busy interstate highway almost directly beneath a sign that said "Camping Prohibited". Turned out we had come up about a half-mile short of the La Costa campground.

The climax of our adventure came early the next morning when Pop said he needed some gas and get some supplies, and he left us there alone with our campsite. It was right along the highway and just above a small beach, and we could see for miles in all directions.

We were almost scared out of our skins when a "hobo"-looking man came out of nowhere and asked us, "Hey boys, do any you of have some extra smokes?" We were eleven and fifteen years old respectively and neither of us smoked, yet for some reason in our situation, it made perfect sense that a hobo who had appeared out of nowhere would be asking us this question at 7:00 a.m. next to a busy highway, adjacent to a camping prohibited sign.

SPRING BREAK TRIP – FINDING MYSELF WITH MY DAUGHTERS

The year was 1986. My wife Bonnie and I along with our two daughters were traveling to Southern California on a spring break trip to visit my father-in-law and his wife in Lancaster, California. The plan was to continue on to Disneyland and San Diego after a few days in Lancaster.

My father-in-law had been diagnosed with cancer and was scheduled to begin chemotherapy soon. It was an opportunity for my wife to spend some time with her father, and a chance for my daughters to visit with and get to know their Grandpa Roy a bit better.

My father-in-law Roy was a rough, gruff and tough retired Army Sergeant and for much of Bonnie's life had been an absent father, either due to his military service or because of his divorce from her mother. But I think the presence of the cancer or of his granddaughters had softened him; he was gentler, warmer and more reflective during this visit than I had ever seen him. It was an important visit, for it was the last time we saw Grandpa Roy. Later that year he died of a heart attack while visiting his family and attending a wedding reception back in his native state of Indiana. My daughters, Adrienne and Erin, were ten and thirteen years old at the time, so the visit provided them with a kind and loving memory of their grandfather.

Bonnie was in the midst of ending her college studies at Sacramento State University and preparing to take the CPA exam. She had contracted a severe cold, so the plan was for us to drop her off at the John Wayne Airport in Orange County, and for my daughters and me to proceed on to the Disneyland Hotel for our Disneyland visit. Then we would travel to San Diego for the rest of the vacation before returning to our home in Sacramento. The girls were very excited about the visit to Disneyland and the time we planned to spend in San Diego visiting the zoo and spending time on the sunny beaches there.

At the time of this trip, I thought of myself as a good father who was involved and supportive of my daughters, and helpful in their schooling and activities. But upon reflection, and in all honesty, I realized their mother was their primary parent in all the major decisions, especially those involving female or girl issues. It was Bonnie who was the one to take charge and guide Adrienne and Erin in those situations. Even though I had grown up in a home with three older sisters, at the time of the trip I had been married for almost twenty years and was living in a household with two daughters, I was like many men – I was clueless about the ways of women and girls. I realize now, in retrospect, how difficult and stressful the world of a single parent can be. Total and complete responsibility for two human beings. Is there a greater responsibility one can have in life? In addition, I realize my identity as a parent and my connection to my daughters had been established moment by moment, day by day, and incident by incident.

I had some apprehension about spending five full days with my daughters without the presence of their mother to serve as the buffer to smooth out any of the rough spots or bumps in the road. I wanted the trip and my time with my daughters to go perfectly; but it did not, and I was reminded that few things in life go perfectly and that it is those imperfect times and challenging times that help to forge the bonds of a strong relationship between parents and their children.

The day we were to spend all day at Disneyland Park started out on the wrong foot, or ankle to be precise, when I sprained my ankle when I stepped in a hole on an early morning run. As soon as I said, "Girls, our day at the park may be in jeopardy" were out of my mouth, the looks on the faces of the girls told me that canceling the day in the park was not an option. I knew I would have to do whatever was necessary, but we would spend the day at the park. And we did. I limped through the visit to

Disneyland, but to my surprise, late in the afternoon my daughters told me they were tired of standing in long lines for the rides and wanted to return to the hotel to spend the rest of the day at the man-made beach there. I will never know if that was a concession on their part to my condition or if they were genuinely tired and wanted to cut short their "dream day in the Magic Kingdom." Whatever the reason, I know that we ended up having a wonderful day at the Disneyland Beach.

The rest of the trip was pretty much the same – the planned activity not turning out exactly as we expected, but we managed to get through it together. Part of our package at the Disneyland Hotel included a day trip to Universal Studios in Los Angeles. On the day of that outing, we learned that a major freeway in Los Angeles was being shut down for the filming of a movie. The fact that this was the first time (and the last time) in history that a major highway was shut down completely for the shooting of a movie, the timing of this event, and others made us wonder about our luck on this trip.

We learned the trip to Universal Studios would go off as planned, only that it would take us twice as long as normal to go from Disneyland to Universal Studios, and our time at the studio would be cut in half. Our bus driver happened to be a part-time actor and aspiring comedian, so he turned our time on the bus to the highlight of our day when he did an ad lib tour of drivers and pedestrians we encountered on the long drive. Although I was disappointed in the shortened time at Universal Studios, all my daughters could talk about was how much fun they had on the bus and how much they were entertained by the funny bus driver.

Our day at the beach in San Diego turned out to be one of the coldest and windiest spring days on record in San Diego, so we had to abandon the beach after about an hour or risk a case of frostbite. In the end, this change in plans afforded us more time at the San Diego Zoo and time for us to explore and get lost numerous times in San Diego. Prior to GPS and cell phones, I learned that relying on ten- and thirteen-year-old navigators who could not clearly read city maps was a way to get to places in San Diego "where no man had gone before."

Although since those days in 1986 I have traveled the world to London, Paris, Rome, Hong Kong, Buenos Aires and other exotic destinations, I have learned that nothing can compare to the adventures of the journey of a clueless dad and his two daughters on a trip that did not go as planned. I came to realize that a trip that might be considered a disaster at the time can actually be the first step in a journey of love that can last a lifetime.

Jim at Facebook Headquarters with Granddaughter Avery and Grandson Cameron

Selfie at Yosemite

*Toasting the Giants with Sister Moe
at Pittsburgh's PNC Ballpark*

*Visiting the Spring Training
Home of the Chicago Cubs in Arizona*

Immigrant – California to Ireland

I am something of a rare breed in California. Not only am I a fourth-generation Californian (on my mother's side), I am also a fourth-generation San Franciscan. I can only imagine what it was like for my ancestors who came from Ireland to California in the 1850s – the hopes, the dreams and the fears that forced them to abandon Ireland as teenagers or young adults and come to a world of unknowns.

In researching my family history in the mid-1990s, I was able to share a bit of this journey in reverse when I returned to Ireland for the very first time. I had been invited to attend a Mullany clan gathering in 1996 in the little town of Boyle, in the County of Roscommon. I knew little of my family history in Ireland, as when I had asked my father about it, he had repeated the words of his own father when he had asked him about Ireland: "Ireland gave us nothing and America gave us everything." My father, who was a first-generation Californian, said that his father and mother had never talked about their life in Ireland, and both of my paternal grandparents died in 1933, the same year my parents had married. So none of my siblings nor I knew anything about the life in the Ireland of my grandparents.

Dublin, Ireland

My journey in Ireland started at a small bed and breakfast inn in Dublin where I had planned to spend a few days sightseeing before heading to Boyle for the clan gathering. As I pulled my rolling suitcase towards the small front desk counter, a smiling middle-aged man greeted me. "Mr. Mullany, please put your bags down and sit a wee bit, as you have come a long way." I was taken by this friendly greeting and wondered how this man knew who I was and why he was making me feel so welcomed. I knew the slogan of the Irish Republic was a Gaelic phrase meaning the land of 10,000 welcomes.

After a bit of chatting and getting acquainted, my host surprised me a bit further by telling me that one of "my people" had arrived. "My people?"

I wondered what he was talking about. As far as I knew, I did not have any people in Ireland. It turned out that another Mullany from America had stopped off at this bed and breakfast a few days before my arrival.

I experienced a bit of the apprehension and fear that all immigrants must feel when I attempted to negotiate the maze that was the Central Dublin train station. I attempted to find the train I needed to board to get to the town of Boyle. The clerk told me I was to board the train heading for "Doonabate" in a language that only vaguely sounded like English. The saying of America and Ireland being two cultures separated by a common language came to mind. He seemed a bit insulted when I asked if he could speak English rather than Gaelic, as I did not understand Gaelic. He then assured me, to my embarrassment, that he was speaking English, and he wrote down the name of the train I needed to take to get to the town of Boyle.

I did make it to the town of Boyle, which is located in the central western area of Ireland. It was a picturesque village with a small river running through it and was situated in the rolling, green Irish countryside. That weekend I would meet more than one hundred of my kin from all over the world: they came from Australia, Canada, English, Scotland, and a good number from throughout Ireland. This was my ancestral home in Ireland and had at one time been called Bally Mullany, or village of the Mullanys. The town turned out to be a Mullany haven, with a Mullany convenience store, a Mullany pub, and even a James

Mullany clothing store. Of course, I had to visit my namesake's clothing store, which was owned by an 85-year old man named James Mullany who still worked every day.

I approached the man and told him my name was also James Mullany and I had come all the way from California to see if I could get a "James Mullany discount." Without cracking a smile, the proprietor replied, "Sorry, no discounts for James Mullanys or anyone else."

By the end of the weekend, I had heard many versions of the same family immigrant story – people who had left Ireland to make better lives for themselves far from their homeland due to the starvation of the potato famine or the lack of economic opportunities in Ireland. Many of their ancestors had participated in the Irish family wake, where young members of the family were sent off across the ocean never to be seen or heard from again by their family and were essentially dead to the family in Ireland. I came to appreciate what it means to be an immigrant and to be drawn away from your homeland by the hope and dream of a better life.

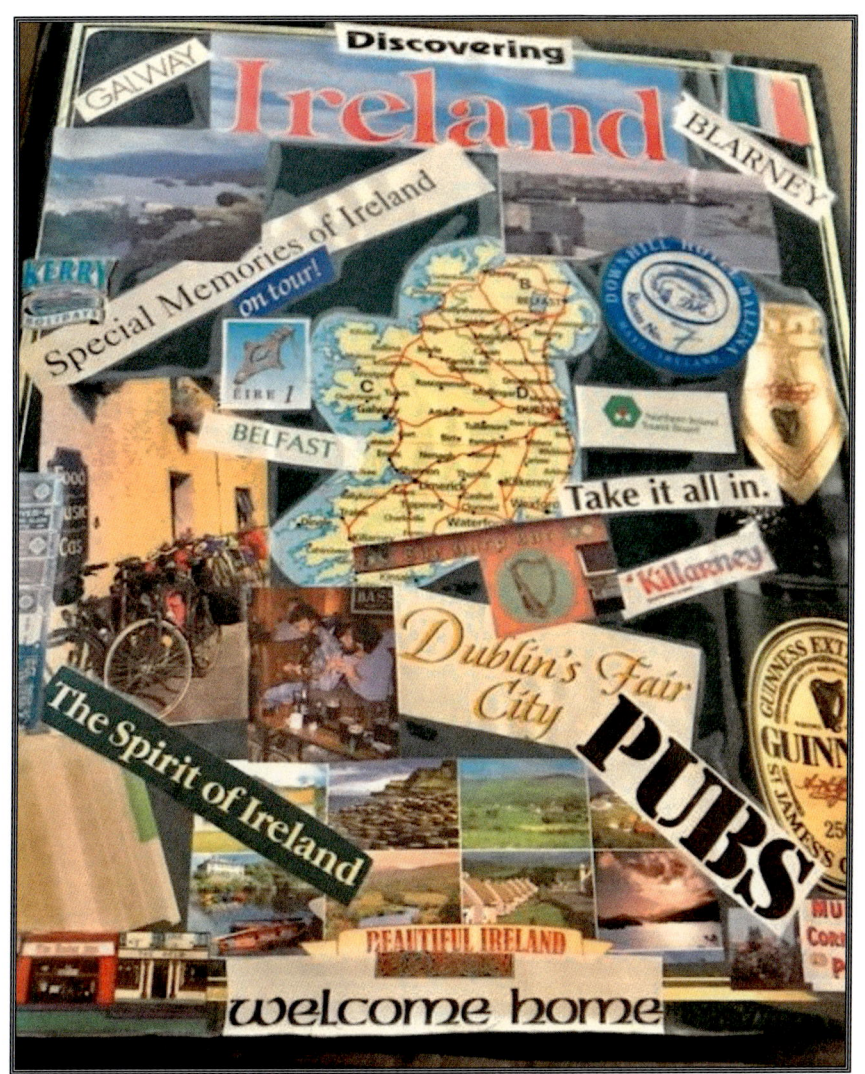

The Good Samaritan and Friends

The Good Samaritan in Ireland

The year was 1995 and I was standing on the deserted railway platform in the rural countryside of Ireland, outside of the town of Boyle in County Roscommon. I was preparing to return to Dublin on a three-hour train trip in preparation for my return to California. The train to Dublin was not scheduled to arrive for more than an hour and a half, the small depot building was locked tight, and there was no sign of life around the station. I was daydreaming a bit as I looked out from my perch on the elevated platform at the rolling emerald green hills surrounding the picturesque village of Boyle a few miles down the road. I had a slight bit of anxiety wondering if the train schedule I had in hand was accurate or if the Irish gift for blarney and for fictional stories extended to train schedules. My mind drifted – forty shades of green, the old sod, and the pints of Guinness I had consumed the previous evening.

My reverie was broken when I noticed that two older ladies had appeared at the end of the platform. I do not refer to them as elderly after having read of a man younger than myself having been referred to by that term. The ladies appeared to be in their late seventies or early eighties and looked like they had walked out of an Irish Victorian novel. From my many years of using public transportation in San Francisco and Sacramento, I usually employed a defensive posture of distance and space in and around public transports to create a self-preservation shell. However, the friendliness and curiosity of these two ladies quickly disarmed me of my usual reluctance to engage with strangers in these settings. After, all I was in rural Ireland, not urban California. We quickly exchanged life histories; I informed them of my journey from California while they enthralled me with the information that they were sisters who were lifetime residents of County Roscommon and this was their very first train trip from this station. The sisters informed me with an infectious enthusiasm that they were traveling on this train to a town just an hour away to visit with their niece who had recently given birth. The train, the station, and the entire venture was a new experience for them. I tried to reassure them with as much information as I had about the train schedule, the ticket purchase process and my conclusion that the depot building would open shortly before the train was scheduled to arrive. I helped them a little bit by carrying their overnight bags.

As people slowly arrived at the platform, the ladies found it necessary to tell each one of the locals about the man from California, and then it was "this good man", and finally they were referring to me as "their good Samaritan." I was not really sure of the context of this biblical parable being applied to me, but I must admit that the ladies making me into a local celebrity had me feeling good and comfortable with these strangers. At this point, the station master arrived and announced that the depot building was now open for business. I accompanied the ladies to a small waiting room through a door that was propped open. For a few minutes, I was basking in all this glory of recognition, thinking how great Ireland was.

My little reverie was suddenly interrupted by the station agent, who approached and told me, "Sir, you must leave immediately." He was a bit gruff and abrupt; I figured that he was not aware that he was talking to "the good man – the Good Samaritan." As I was thinking of a suitable response to the man, I looked over his shoulder and saw the door that had been propped open was slowly closing. The sign affixed to the door read "Women's Lounge." I quickly gathered up my luggage and what remained of my dignity and retreated back out to the platform. I think the last thing I heard was a few subdued chuckles coming from the Ladies Lounge.

Guinness is Good for Jim

Good Samaritan Railway Station

LETTERS TO MY GRANDCHILDREN

"Letter writing is the only device for combining solitude with good company."
George Gordon Noel Byron

BECOMING POPPA

I was never one of those parents who put any pressure on my daughters to have children for the sake of giving me a grandchild. First, by the time my daughters were married, they had long ago stopped listening to any suggestions or advice I could give them. I was very confident that both of them knew what they wanted out of their lives and I felt it was none of my business whether or not they should choose to have children. I was somewhat neutral on the subject of grandchildren; if they chose to have children it would be fine with me, and if they chose not to have children, that was fine too.

Everything changed when my daughter Adrienne gave birth to Avery Kendall Jones on June 14, 2007. For me, it was love at first sight. A few days after Avery was born I was able to hold her, and when she looked up at me she had me – I was madly in love with this baby girl, even when at this point in her life her only accomplishments were that she could burp and her toothless smile was really just a reaction to having gas. I did not care, for in my eyes it was the greatest burp in the history of babies, and her gas had the fragrance of the most expensive perfume.

I learned that the relationship between a grandparent and a grandchild was one of total and complete unconditional love. We had no expectations or obligations, so we were freely able to appreciate and delight in each other on the most basic level. I especially liked the fact that neither of us could care less about what others thought or felt about us. If we wanted to go gaga over each other, that was our business.

A few years later, Avery introduced me to the fact that she was going have a little brother when she wore a shirt that said: "I am Going to Be a Big Sister." Thus, in February of 2009, "little brother," or younger brother Cameron Dominick Jones, became the second grandchild, and he was a big boy at over ten pounds at birth. Cameron quickly acquired the nickname of Mr. C. Just like Avery, Cameron was loved unconditionally by his family and by his grandparents, too, although when he was born, Avery found the rocking chair in her mom's hospital room far more interesting than Cameron.

The grandchildren family roster was completed in 2011 when my daughter Erin gave birth to grandson Ian James in a rather unconventional manner. Ian was born in the twenty-sixth week of Erin's pregnancy and entered the world weighing just two pounds six ounces. Ian spent three months in the neonatal intensive care unit and was clearly a miracle baby. My connection to Ian James was strengthened by the fact we shared the name James.

The idea for writing letters to my grandchildren came from two sources. First, it came from a suggestion in the book called Wonderful Ways to Love a Grandchild. The second source was Jack Gallagher, a Sacramento comedian and actor, who wrote letters to his son Declan, that became his wonderful stage show, "Letters to Declan."

A Letter To Avery

June 14, 2007

Hello Baby Avery,

    Today was one of the happiest days of my life because you came into the world. I cannot express how happy the news of your birth makes me. I guess I need to introduce myself – I am your Poppa Jim, or James Leo Mullany. I am the father of your mother, Adrienne Colleen Jones (Mullany). I am sure that in the future you will find out how lucky you are to be born to parents that will love you deeply, protect you and care for you all of your life. Your mom and dad, Adrienne and Joel Jones, are very kind, caring and sensitive people who will love and support you.

    Today you surprised all of us by arriving so early. We did not expect that you would be born until around July 23rd, but I guess you could not wait because you arrived more than a month early. What a wonderful surprise you were! I like it when people arrive early, and you will learn as you grow up that some people in our family are early and others are late. I hope that you are one of the early people, but we will love you no matter whether you are an early bird or a late person.

    At around 7:30 this morning I had a telephone call from your dad, and he told me that he and your mom were at Good Samaritan Hospital in San Jose and that it looked like you would be born today. All of us in your family who heard the news were a bit nervous and afraid because it seemed too early for you to arrive, and we were a little bit worried that something may have been wrong with you or your mom. Your dad, Joel, was very calm and reassuring when he told me that everything was all right and the doctors were confident that you would be born healthy. I was so happy when, later in the afternoon, I received a call from your mom telling me that you had been born; you were a five-pound, fourteen-ounce baby girl who was nineteen inches long, and you had blue eyes and blond hair. I was so happy that I cried – you were my very first grandchild. Your mom is kind of quiet, but I could tell that she was very happy and pleased because she smiled and her eyes twinkled. I have known her since she was born, so you can trust me on this.

Because you arrived early, your mom and dad did not have enough time to even pick out a name for you. I later heard that they had narrowed down the choice of your name to either Gabriella or Avery. I hope that you are happy with your name. I am sure someday your mom and dad will tell you how they decided to name you Avery Kendall Jones. But whatever reasons your parents had, we are very happy you have such a beautiful name.

Once I heard you had been born and that you and your mom were healthy, I could not think of anything else – just you. I am living in Pacific Grove, which is about fifty miles away from your new home in San Jose, but I wanted to get into my car right away and drive to the hospital to see you. But because you were born early and they wanted to check you out and make sure you were okay, I had to wait awhile to visit you and your mom. I visited you the next day, and I think I was the very first visitor you had at the hospital.

I want you to know that there will always be people in your life who will love you unconditionally, which means that no matter what happens – good or bad, happy or sad, success or failure – your family will always love you. That is important for you to know right from the start of your life – knowing your family loves you no matter what.

With love,
POPPA

Avery Jones is now a 6th grader in middle school. She loves school and excels in math, science and she loves to read. She runs on the cross-country team and also plays volleyball.

A Letter To Cameron

Cameron Jones

June 17, 2010

Dear Cameron,

    You are now sixteen months old, so I wanted to start writing you some letters that you can read when you are older. I love you so much and am happy that I am your Poppa. You are the first boy that has been born into the Mullany family. Your Grammy and I had two girls – your mom, Adrienne and your Aunt Erin. Then the first child your mom had was your sister Avery. I think it will be a lot of fun for us to play sports like baseball and basketball when you get older. If you don't like those sports that will be okay too. Also, we share the same birthday month; I was born on February 3rd and you were born on February 17th – just few years apart (I was born in 1945 and you were born in 2009). I am not real great at math, so when you are older you can figure out the difference in our ages. Last weekend, your family had a birthday party for your sister Avery to celebrate her 3rd birthday and you called me Poppa for the first time. You pointed at me and said, "Poppa." I cannot explain to you how happy that made me feel.

    A few months ago, I had a stroke; that is when your brain has a problem because it does not get enough blood. It scared me and I had to go to the hospital in an ambulance. When I heard the word stroke, one of the first things I thought about was you and your sister Avery and how I wanted to see and share the big events of your lives – like seeing your graduations from school, watching your big sporting events and games, playing sports with you and Avery and attending all your birthday parties as you grow up. Those are things that grandparents want to see and be part of, and I hope I live a long time to see all of those things.

    I want to share with you a few things that I have learned in my life, so they might help you in some way with your life. *True* or *real* love is unconditional. That means that when you love someone, you love him or her even when they make mistakes or when they do things that you think they should not do. Remember, we all make mistakes.

Remember to believe in yourself and do not let others tell you what you can or cannot do in your life. Also, as you go through life don't be afraid to make mistakes or get things wrong. I think in some ways we learn more from our mistakes and failures than we do by our successes.

Finally, remember to have fun. Sometimes we get so serious about things that we forget to laugh, smile and do things for fun and happiness. Try not to be a worrier. I know that I have spent a lot of time worrying about things that never happen. There is a funny song I like – "Don't Worry, Be Happy."

Never forget there are people in your life who always love you. Your mom and dad will always love you and be there for you whenever you need help. Sometimes they will make you mad or upset you (that is what parents do) but they always will love you. Don't forget to tell them you love them too.

Be kind to animals. You have a sweet dog named Roxy. Be good to her and other animals.

AND ALWAYS REMEMBER, POPPA LOVES YOU!!!

Cameron Jones is a fourth grader and does very well in school. He loves sports and plays on the soccer and basketball teams. His favorite basketball player is Stephen Curry of the Warriors.

A Letter To Ian James

Dear Ian James,

      Do you believe in miracles? I certainly do because so far, your life has been a miracle to all of your family. On July 4, 2013, you will be two years old. I am not sure how old you will be when you read this letter, but I want you to know that your life is truly a miracle. Each time you say to me "Poppa, Poppa," I feel a happiness and joy that I cannot put into words. Whenever I see you, I feel things that I cannot adequately describe.

      On July 4, 2011, I received a telephone call from your Momma (as you call her now) informing me that she had delivered a baby boy, "Ian Scarborough," and that you weighed just about two pounds and six ounces, and that you had been born in the twenty-sixth week of her pregnancy. Later, she told me that she and your dad had added the middle name "James" to your name in honor of Poppa – me. I was just so honored! I think that because we share the name "James" we are linked together in a very special way – forever. The name James connects us with a link to my grandfather who was named James White and to my father who was named James Joseph Mullany.

      I must admit that at first, I was very scared for you and your parents because you were so tiny. In order to survive, you had all these wires, tubes and monitors attached to your tiny body and you needed intensive care in the hospital for three months, including a heart procedure. You needed help to breathe, help with feeding and special help to keep your body warm; you needed the help of a team of doctors, nurses and medical specialists so you could grow sufficiently to be able to go home in early October. But even with all of these scares, the first time I saw you in your incubator or 'pod unit', I saw that special look in your eyes, and knowing the love, spirit, and devotion of your parents, I knew that you would not only survive but you would thrive, and I just felt that you would grow to become the very special boy that you have grown to become.

      Even though you had great care by a wonderful team of doctors, nurses and specialists and the very best of modern medical technology, I am convinced that the most important thing you had (and still have) is the love, devotion, and dedication of your parents. While you were in the neonatal intensive care unit at the Kaiser Hospital in Roseville, California, each and every day one or both of your parents were there with you. Some days, either your mama or daddy would come two or three times to be with you, to help care for you, and to hold you for many hours. I think it was their presence, care, touch and love that helped you survive more than anything else. The times I was there with you, I saw your eyes just light up and your body relax whenever your mama or daddy would pick you up and hold you. Something very magical and special happened whenever they touched you – love and healing were taking place.

     As you grow up, I am sure you will hear many stories about the time when you were a micro preemie in the neonatal intensive care unit. I want you to always remember that it was the love, dedication, care and support of your mama and daddy that were the most important factors in your survival. They held you and warmed you with their bodies for many hours; they were there to care for you and to make sure that you received all the attention and treatment you needed. During your life, you will read and hear stories about courageous heroes and people to be admired, but remember you will not have to look any farther than your own parents to see the real heroes in your life. Please don't ever forget that, and always remember:

Ian James, we all love you!

Ian James Scarborough, Age 6
Ian James Scarborough is a happy and healthy first grader, after having been born 3 months prematurely and weighing just over 2 pounds. And just like his Poppa, he loves baseball and played on 2 teams (the Angels and the Junior Giants).

The Cousins
Avery, Cameron and Ian James

BEGINNINGS AND ENDINGS

*"Sometimes things fall apart,
so that better things can fall together"*
Marilyn Monroe

My Story – Hitting Rock Bottom

    I wondered if Bruce Springsteen, Woody Allen, Gwyneth Paltrow, John Lennon David Lettermen, Lady Gaga, Johnny Carson and Robin Williams all hit rock bottom in the same way I had, for we all shared a serious problem.

    From as far back in my life as I could remember, I had been a worrier. I worried about big things and small things – school results, sports team's games and even that fat, bald-headed Russian guy they showed on television during the cold war who said he wanted to bury us. My earliest worries had to do with test results and grades, but I recall I worried about whether I would be called upon by the teacher to go up to the blackboard and show how I had solved a math problem, or whether I would be called upon by the priest who came to our classroom to quiz us on the catechism. As I advanced in school from elementary to high school, the stakes and outcomes became even more important, the worries became more pronounced and added to the mix, anxiety that produced more physical reactions. I was worried about getting the grades and the test results that would get me into college, which was viewed as the critical next step in a college preparatory high school. Included in the college goal was the reality that I would have to earn the money necessary for college tuition., as my father was unable to assist me in paying for college.

    I proceeded through college, then there was the military draft, the Vietnam War and my service in the Air Force, where dying in the war became a distinct possibility. More and more things to worry about and have anxiety about. I recall my father's advice about worrying: "Most of the things people worry about never happen, or those "big events" we worry about are quickly forgotten within a few months or a year" – as in, within a year, you won't even remember these things you had worried about

As I went into my thirties I had a family, and it was a mortgage and a career that became my focus. For much of my life, running had been a stress reliever for me; at times, I did achieve the runner's high, but most of the time the act of running and the fatigue it produced relaxed me and was a form of meditation that freed my brain of tension and anxiety. As I grew older, though, something more disturbing had entered my mind and my life like a thief in the night, a feeling of being blue or sad, an anxiety that overwhelmed me and took over my life. I had periods when I had an empty feeling of hopelessness and worthlessness, a feeling that made me irritable and restless. At the time, the idea or concept of biorhythms had become popular or trendy – biorhythms – a cycle of ups and downs a person went through as a natural and normal cycle of life that all people experienced. So, for a time I thought I was experiencing a cycle of biorhythms. But then I realized there was more to it than that. I lost all interest in my usual pleasurable activities like reading, hiking, watching my favorite sports teams play. At first, I thought there was something seriously wrong with me and so I did what many men do, I pretended it did not exist and I hid it from my family and friends. I am not sure when I first heard about depression being a major disorder. But during the early stages of the condition, I just lived with it and rationalized it was a normal reaction to life events or ailments or some side effect of the medication.

Before I realized it, about twenty years had passed and regular bouts of depression were just a part of my life. However, subconsciously I realized that I had a good life, and the depression was not logically connected to my life; when I should have been happy and proud, I was depressed and sad. Out of shame or fear of having what was considered to be a mental illness, I did my best to hide my condition from family and friends. As painful as the condition may have been, the fear of others knowing I had it was even more fearful. The only therapist I trusted with my secret was my wife Bonnie. I somehow only shared my pain with her, and I made it her job to somehow make me feel better, to make me feel happy.

Without realizing it until it was too late, I had unknowingly burdened her with the role that was almost even more painful than my own – she had to be a listener, confidante, and co-conspirator in my effort to keep my condition secret. It was an impossible burden to inflict upon another, much less upon the person you loved and trusted above all others. Throughout the years, I continued to fail to heed her advice to seek outside help. It was out of fear or shame, and just because this was an element of the condition for most men. The fear of being thought of as being weak or mentally ill by others outflanked the logic of getting help, which would have been a logical step had it just been a physical ailment.

I was stunned in the winter of 1995 when Bonnie announced that she planned on leaving me at the beginning of the New Year. As in the breakup of any marriage, especially one that was in its twenty-seventh year, there are many factors leading to the breakup. In ours, my depression was a major factor, although Bonnie never made my seeking help as a condition that would keep us together. I pleaded with her about seeking marriage counseling, but I knew that before making a decision so serious as this one, Bonnie would have explored all options, and with her, there would be no going back. If I thought I was depressed before her departure, a few days after New Year's Day in 1996, I knew the worst was to come as I heard her car pull out of the driveway on that winter afternoon. My world was shattered, as I was one of those people who still believed marriage was forever and I had failed in the most important relationship of my life.

The next few weeks I lived in a fog, just going through the motions of life without any thought of what I was doing. I had been married since I was twenty-three years old. I knew of no other life as an adult. Fortunately, my daughter Adrienne was away at college and daughter Erin was gone from the house almost every day with school and work. Each moment it was a physical and mental struggle just to move one foot in front of the other. I had heard many men buried themselves in work when faced with a crisis in their life. In my case that was not an option either, as I was part of a state office which had become toxic as one of my supervisors was being investigated for having a created a hostile work environment, which she certainly had done. I was literally living life in a fog.

My work situation was resolved to my satisfaction, and it turned from the worst of working conditions I had ever experienced to the very best when I was given my dream assignment of implementing the statewide voluntary paternity program. The depression persistently haunted me. It did not make sense. The program reached the ultimate zenith of recognition when it was featured on the front page of the Los Angeles Times Sunday edition, yet in a matter of weeks, I would hit rock bottom.

Despite the Paternity Program's success and my personal recognition of receiving a state-wide award and being invited to present workshops all over the country, the depression and my sadness seemed to get worse rather than better. At a key point in the project, I had to inform my supervisor that I needed time off to deal with a problem (without being specific about what it was). My boss, Bill, was by far the best supervisor I had in my thirty-plus years of working with the state. Bill calmly said he had such trust and faith in me that if I needed time off, I could have all I needed, as he knew I would not have made this request unless the problem had been serious. I won't be so dramatic as to say his actions of giving me time off saved my life, but they did come close to that. Granting me time off likely meant more work for him and for my unit. I don't think I ever reached the extreme of being suicidal, but I was questioning the reason and purpose of my life.

My initial plan was to use this time off to finally address my problem of depression, but I used the first week of time off to procrastinate and to withdraw myself from social contacts. I hardly left my house except to walk the dog and buy some food. I did not answer the phone, nor did I call anyone. I was a recluse that week. On the second week, one morning I was in bed and my dog, Lady, was by the bed staring up at me. Her sad, brown eyes said to me, "If I could drive a car or open the door I would be out of here, just like the other ladies in the family." Although I did not realize it at the time, looking back on it, I had hit rock bottom. My only social contact was with a dog, and in my mind, even that dog was questioning me. Even though I had walked the mean streets of San Francisco as a fraud investigator, had served four years in the Air Force and had participated in sports all of my life, picking up that phone and making the call to the mental health clinic may have been the most courageous act in my life.

I recall skulking and sneaking to my first appointment at the clinic in Roseville, California, worrying that someone I knew would see me going to "the clinic." But after that first appointment, a rapid whirlwind with a couple of more appointments, and a prescription, the darkness and weight were finally lifted from me, and in a torrent, I began to experience life. I received some awards for my work in the Paternity Program, but more importantly, I came to fully enjoy the process of working with the people who implemented the program throughout California – birth clerks at all of California's birthing hospitals, county vital statistic registrars and even child support attorneys.

Then it was retirement – reading, writing and running. The joy of following my heart and dreams of moving to the beautiful central coast city of Pacific Grove where I did not know a soul and learning that a town that celebrated the return of monarch butterflies with a kid's parade was a perfect fit for me. And there was even a nice writing class just a short walk away.

Just as the lows and sadness of depression came suddenly, so do the discoveries and highs of traveling – London, Paris, Rome, Barcelona, Dublin, Hong Kong, New Zealand, Australia, South America, Saint Petersburg, Budapest, Prague, and all the wonderful people I met along the way. And those ultimate joys – walking my younger daughter Adrienne down the aisle of the Carmel Mission on her wedding day, and walking my older daughter Erin across the sands of a spectacular beach in Kauai in Hawaii – even having another dog of my daughters come into my life and greeting me with her full body wag which said to me, "You are an all right guy and I want to hang out with you," to the ultimate joys of grandchildren Avery and Cameron – **"We love you, Poppa**! and of course, the baseball joys of hearing, "**The Giants won the Pennant, the Giants won the Pennant, the Giants won the pennant!"**

But as we all learn, with or without depression, life is not all highs and joys. There are real lows and sadness too – a stroke, a cancer scare, a hip replacement and the loss of a best friend. And the terrifying period of my daughter going into premature labor three months early and the birth of a two-pound bundle of joy named Ian James, and his life and death battle for three months in intensive care and his survival is all we can think about, and to see him emerge – **"I love you, Poppa!"**

I could not believe it had been almost twenty years since I made that phone call to the clinic in Roseville. And how grateful I was for the life I was given without the depression, anxiety and the sadness. But never say never, for in the late fall of 2015, a familiar though distant feeling reemerged when I had a feeling of a malaise or lack of motivation that seemed to turn into the holiday blues between Thanksgiving and Christmas. I just found myself unmotivated, with an undercurrent of sadness. And before I had even realized it, the old pattern had returned – denial and a bit of shame. It had been years since I had taken any medication for the condition. It was time to celebrate the holidays and I did not feel like buying presents, attending parties and celebrating. I was going thru the motions – pretending, putting on a good front. Even the trip to Sacramento for the annual joyous Christmas celebration with my daughters, grandchildren, and Bonnie seemed like a chore.

    It did not take Bonnie long to recognize the façade I was putting up, and she pulled me aside on Christmas Eve and told me that my daughters had recognized the signs also and they were concerned about me. Fortunately, my grandchildren were too young to see these signs in Poppa. I realized that I needed to address the situation as soon as possible or I might be dragging down our Christmas holiday celebration. One of the changes in my medical coverage from twenty years ago was that I could e-mail my doctor and have him approve a prescription in a matter of hours, which is what I did. So, on Christmas Day I was able to go to a clinic and pick up my prescription present, and I had reason to celebrate a Merry Christmas and a very Happy New Year. Joy to the World!

BEFORE I DIE, I WANT TO ...

Back in June of 2006 when I retired from my career with the State of California in Sacramento, I think, without even being aware of it, I set forth my **"Before I Die, I Want To…"** list. As do many people embarking on retirement, I had my list of "Before I die, I Want To or I Will Do". Some items on my list were those dreams we all have but oftentimes think will never happen; others were informal plans as to how my life was going to be once I had the time to do those things I never had the time or money to do when I was working and raising a family.

First, as a native San Franciscan who had spent the first quarter of his life living on a peninsula in the city of San Francisco, it was a secret dream of mine to move to Pacific Grove on the beautiful Monterey Peninsula, the area I had always loved to visit. Before I die, I want to – **Move to Pacific Grove – Check! Mission accomplished** in 2007 when I moved to Pacific Grove.

I had always had an interest in my Irish heritage and ancestry and wanted to visit Ireland. My father and mother, whose families had both come from Ireland, had not been able to visit Ireland in their lifetime, so it was on their behalf I wanted to visit Ireland. **Three Visits to Ireland. Check! Mission accomplished.** And out of those visits, a foundation and dream for more travel grew and was nurtured by trips to Australia, New Zealand, South America, Europe, China, the Baltic Region, Scandinavia, and the great cities of the world, London, Paris, Berlin, Hong Kong, Sydney. Before I die I want to – **Travel the World – Check! Mission Accomplished.**

Before I die I want to leave a legacy or history of my family to my children and grandchildren in my writings. What originated as a formal genealogical family history evolved into a series of writings that I call *Jim's Jottings – Telling My Stories and Sharing My Memories*, thanks to Illia Thompson's memoir writing class in Pacific Grove and Carmel. Before I die, I want a **Legacy of my writings for my children and grandchildren – Check! Mission Still in Progress.**

Before I die, I wanted to give something back to my lifelong passions that have given me so much in my lifetime. Through volunteer work at the Roseville, California Animal Shelter, the Pacific Grove Public Library's Author Committee and the St. Angela's Food Closet and Distribution Programs, I have been able to give back and receive so much in return from things I am passionate about. Before I die, **I want to give something to my passions and in gratitude for so much that I have been given in return – Check! Mission Accomplished.**

Early in the morning in late January 2010, while I was being transported to the Emergency Room at the Community Hospital of the Monterey Peninsula, my own mortality came into focus for the first time in my life. I had awakened that morning feeling very strange, with awkwardness and tingling in my left arm and hand; I stumbled into the wall when I tried to walk to the bathroom. I knew something was just not right. In response to my 911 call, a team of firemen paramedics and ambulance Emergency Medical Technicians arrived within ten minutes of my call. And after a short period of diagnosis and evaluation, I was wheeled out to the ambulance for the trip to the hospital. On that ride to the hospital, I heard that dreaded word – Stroke. I was scared because I was unsure of the severity of the stroke and the impact it would have on my life. During that ride to the hospital, I faced the real possibility that I might die in the near future.

As I rode in the ambulance, my mind raced and I pondered my mortality. My first thought was I wanted to live to see and share in the lives of my grandchildren Avery and Cameron, who were both under the age of three years at the time. I thought before I die, I want to watch their games, their school plays, their highs and their lows, their graduations and as many of their milestones as I can. Their young lives had brought me unbelievable joy and happiness, and I wanted for them to know the love of their Poppa as they grew up. I think I was surprised that I had these positive thoughts as the ambulance approached the hospital. I think in some ways my stroke and the ride to the hospital happened for this reason, to remind me what was truly important in my life.

As it turned out, the stroke was deemed "minor" by the medical professionals, and with great relief, I learned there would be no residual side-effects. Later, I was so grateful for the fact that I have been able to be around for the miraculous birth of one more grandchild, Ian James, who came into the world three months premature on July 4, 2011, and he has brought even more love, happiness, and joy into the lives of our family.

I have been so blessed, and I appreciate every moment I have been gifted with to enjoy so many "Before I Die" moments with Avery, Cameron, and Ian James.

ACKNOWLEDGMENTS

I first wish to thank my parents, Jim and Lucille Mullany, and my siblings Ann, Maureen, Lucille, and Mike for providing me with all the material a writer might ever need for a lifetime of writing, along with the Irish ability to tell stories with a bit of humor, blarney and pain that is a part of all the Irish. I want also to thank my daughters Erin Jennifer (Mullany) Scarborough and Adrienne Colleen (Mullany) Jones along with husbands Leo Scarborough and Joel Jones along with granddaughter Avery Kendall Jones and grandsons Cameron Dominick Jones and Ian James Scarborough, and for their love, support, fun and the joy they brought to my life as dad and as Poppa. Also, I would like to thank Bonnie Jean Mullany for our over twenty years of marriage and friendship and her devoted time as mother and role model to our daughters and her Grammy time to the grandchildren. (Also, for those great (secret family recipe) butter horn rolls for the holidays)

I especially wish to thank Marnie Sperry for her awesome technical and editorial skills – and also for her gentle encouragement and support. Of course, I want to thank Illia Thompson and my classmates both at the Sally Griffin Center in Pacific Grove and at the Carmel Foundation in Carmel for being both an inspiration to write and for giving me a safe and supportive environment in which to write. Illia was not only a facilitator of writing, but over time a person that I regard as a friend. I want to especially thank classmates Barbara Moody, Christine Henrard, Margaret McHuugh and Natalya Livingston for their kind words about my writing and their encouragement to stick with it.

Also, thanks to Jeannie Gould and Kathy Nielsen, for sharing their experience and knowledge regarding the process of actually producing and book.

I want to thank classmate Pat Moyer for his friendship and his writing assistance? (which was of dubious value). During our after-class lunches at the Swiss Café in Carmel we could pretend in our discussions that we were real writers; that also provided us with hours of useless discussion about San Francisco television trivia, along with our parochial high school and State College and government employment experiences.

Finally, I would like to thank my "Cover Crew" and coffee drinking pals: Alex Barth, The Tech Man; Cherie Rousseau, The Artist and; Tom Heebink, The Publicist and Craft Beer Consultant.

Author Jim Mullany with his family, 2018 in Pacific Grove, CA

ABOUT THE AUTHOR

James (Jim) Mullany was born and raised in San Francisco, California. He graduated from San Francisco State College in the late 1960s. Following his graduation, he served an enlistment in the United States Air Force. He worked for the State of California for thirty-eight years both as Special Investigator for the Employment Department and as a Program Analyst for Social Services and the State's Paternity Program in Sacramento. He has two grown daughters and three grandchildren. He currently resides in Pacific Grove, California.

In *Baseball, Bobbleheads and Beyond*, Jim Mullany has written a series of essays about growing up in San Francisco, his Irish Catholic family, baseball, and his other passions in life. In keeping with his Irish heritage, the stories are infused with humor, emotion and poignancy.

Made in the USA
Middletown, DE
30 August 2019